# David MacLennan

FOLK
LORE
PUBLISHING

The Publisher: Folklore Publishing
Website: www.folklorepublishing.com

Library and Archives Canada Cataloguing in Publication

MacLennan, David, 1977–
    Jokes for Canadian kids / David MacLennan.

ISBN 978-1-926677-45-3

    1. Canadian wit and humor (English). 2. Riddles, Juvenile. 3. Canada—Humor—Juvenile literature. I. Title.

PS8375.M34 2011          jC818'.602          C2010-906278-7


Project Director: Faye Boer
Project Editor: Kathy van Denderen
Proofreader: Tracey Comeau
Production: Kerri Kenny, HR Media Group
Cover Image: Courtesy of © 2007 Jupiter Images

Produced with the assistance of the Government of Alberta, Alberta Multimedia Development Fund.

**Government of Alberta** ■

We acknowledge the financial support of the Government of Canada through the Canada Book Fund (CBF) for our publishing activities.

 Canadian    Patrimoine
Heritage     canadien

PC: 1

# Contents

# Introduction

Being funny isn't easy, but when you can find that sweet spot deep inside someone's mind and tickle their funny bone, it's one of the best feelings on the planet.

If laughter is the best medicine, then my prescription for you is to read five pages a day. This book is chock full of gut-splitting, face-hurting, mind-boggling, brain-twisting, tear-inducing hilarious jokes that are sure to get you and your friends laughing. Humour is everywhere; it's in your school, on the playground, in the cafeteria and even in math class.

Adults are too busy worrying about…well…they worry about everything and don't take the time to notice just how funny the world is.

Food is funny. Fish are funny: "Two fish are in a tank. One turns to the other and says, 'Do you know how to drive this thing?'"

Sports are full of funny flubs and bad teams. Just ask the Toronto Maple Leafs; they've been a joke for decades.

Even your lazy cat and crazy dog can tell a good joke every now and again, but you have to listen carefully.

Humour is everywhere in the world. You just need to know where to look. So take this book with you wherever you go and carry a little laughter around.

## CHAPTER ONE

# Higher Education

"What time does the library open?" the man on the phone asks.

"Nine AM," came the reply. "And what's the idea of calling me at home in the middle of the night to ask a question like that?"

"Not until nine AM?" the man said in a disappointed voice.

"No, not till nine AM!" the librarian said. "Why do you want to get in before nine AM?"

"Who said I wanted to get in?" the man said with a sigh. "I want to get out."

"How do you say your ABCs backwards?" asks the teacher to her class.

Johnny, the troublemaker of the class, stands up immediately, and replies, "Why, you would say CBA, Teacher."

Teacher: "According to the ancient Greek scholar Archimedes, what happens when a body is immersed in water?"

Elizabeth: "Usually, the phone rings."

# Homework Excuses

To get things started and to prepare you for the school year, we have gathered all the best excuses that you will need when you have to explain to your teacher why your homework isn't done:

- I put it in a safe but lost the combination.

- My dog ate it.

- My cat tore it to pieces.

- My Pokémon zapped it.

- The air pollution was so bad that my eyes kept tearing, and I couldn't read a thing.

- I lost it fighting this kid who said you weren't the best teacher in the school.

- I didn't do it because I didn't want to add to your already heavy workload.

- Our furnace stopped working, and we had to burn it to stop ourselves from freezing.

- I didn't do it because I didn't want the other kids in the class to look bad.

- Terrorists kidnapped me, and they only just let me go, so I didn't have time to do it.

- I left it in my shirt, and my mother put it in the washing machine.

- And the favourite and unbelievably true reason for not doing homework and missing school happened in the summer of 2009 when U.S. President Barack Obama made a stop in Green Bay, Wisconsin. When John Corpus stood to ask Obama a question, he told the president that his daughter was missing school to attend the event.

  Hearing this, Obama asked, "Do you need me to write a note?" The crowd laughed, but Obama was serious.

  On a piece of paper, the president inscribed, "To Kennedy's teacher: Please excuse Kennedy's absence. She's with me. Barack Obama."

  Kennedy said she would frame the note and give her teacher a copy.

A young student named Michael reports for a final examination that consists of only true/false questions. Michael takes a seat in the classroom, stares at the test for five minutes, removes a coin from his pocket and starts tossing the coin and marking the answer sheet. Heads means "true," tails means "false." He finishes the exam in 30 minutes, while the rest of the class is sweating it out. Suddenly, during the last few minutes of the test, Michael begins desperately tossing the coin in the air and sweating profusely.

The moderator, alarmed, approaches Michael and asks him what is going on.

"Well, I finished the exam in half an hour," replies Michael, "but I thought I ought to recheck my answers."

Father to his son: "Let me see your report card."

Son: "My friend just borrowed it. He wants to scare his parents."

Little Timmy is on a school trip to the local church. On the walls of the large cathedral, he sees beautiful stained glass windows depicting men dressed in uniforms and armour. He asks a nearby priest who the men are.

"Those are our boys who died in service of the church," replies the priest.

Little Timmy asks, "Was that the morning service or the evening service?"

Maria walks into her science class and finds that the new teacher has put five birds on a table and covered them so only their feet showed.

"What's this?" Maria asks the teacher.

"It's an exam," explains the teacher. "Your job is to identify each bird by looking at its feet."

"What a stupid test!" yells out Maria.

Angered, the teacher yells back, "What's your name?!"

Instantly, Maria pulls up her pant legs and answers, "You tell me."

Son: "I can't go to school today."
Father: "Why not?"
Son: "I don't feel well."
Father: "Where don't you feel well?"
Son: "In school!"

Teacher: "Are you good at math?"
Pupil: "Yes and no."
Teacher: "What do you mean?"
Pupil: "Yes, I'm no good at math!"

It is at the end of the school year, and a kindergarten teacher is receiving gifts from her pupils.

Q: What do elves learn in school?
A: The elf-abet.

The florist's son hands her a gift. She shakes it, holds it over her head, and says, "I bet I know what it is. Some flowers."

"That's right," the boy says, "but how did you know?"

"Oh, just a wild guess," she replies.

The next pupil is the candy shop owner's daughter.

The teacher holds her gift overhead, shakes it, and says, "I bet I can guess what it is. A box of sweets."

"That's right, but how did you know?" asks the girl.

"Oh, just a wild guess," replies the teacher.

The next gift is from the son of a liquor store owner.

The teacher holds the package overhead, but it is leaking. She touches a drop of the leakage with her finger and places it to her tongue. "Is it wine?" she asks.

"No," the boy replies, with some excitement.

The teacher repeats the process, taking a larger drop of the leakage to her tongue. "Is it champagne?" she asks.

"No," the boy replies, with more excitement.

The teacher takes one more taste before declaring, "I give up. What is it?"

With great glee, the boy replies, "It's a puppy!"

Teacher: "Where is the English Channel?"
Pupil: "I don't know. My TV doesn't pick it up."

Mother: "What did you learn in school today?"
Son: "Not enough. I have to go back tomorrow."

As a new school principal, Mr. Mitchell is checking over his school on the first day. Passing the stockroom, he is startled to see the door wide open and teachers bustling in and out, carrying off books and supplies in preparation for the arrival of students the next day. The school where he had been a principal the previous year had used a checkout system only slightly less elaborate than that at Fort Knox.

Cautiously, he asks the school's long-time custodian, "Do you think it's wise to keep the stockroom unlocked and to let the teachers take things without requisitions?"

The custodian looks at the principal gravely and replies, "We trust them with the children, don't we?"

One morning a mother is called to pick up her son at the school nurse's office. When she walks through the main entrance, she notices a woman who has curlers in her hair and is wearing pajamas.

"Why are you dressed like that?" the mother asks the woman.

"I told my son that if he ever did anything to embarrass me, I would embarrass him right back," she explains. "He was caught cutting school. So now I've come to spend the day with him!"

A new kid at a very exclusive school in Toronto is looking for the library. He comes across an older student and asks, "Excuse me, I'm new here. Do you know where the library is at?"

The older student looks the kid over with a glare and replies, "At this school, we never end a sentence with a preposition."

"Sorry," says the new kid. "Where's the library at, jerk?"

Q: What did the ghost teacher say to her class?

A: Watch the board, and I'll go through it again.

A geography teacher is doing a lecture on map reading. After explaining about latitude, longitude, degrees and minutes, the teacher asks the class, "Suppose I asked you to meet me for lunch at 23 degrees, 4 minutes north latitude, and 45 degrees, 15 minutes east longitude?"

After a confused silence, little Johnny volunteers, "I guess you'd be eating alone!"

## Kid Logic

A first-grade teacher collects well-known proverbs. She gives each child in her class the first half of a proverb and asks them to come up with the remainder. The students' insight may surprise you:

- Better to be safe than...punch a fifth grader.
- It's always darkest before...daylight savings.
- You can lead a horse to water but...how?
- Don't bite the hand that...looks dirty.
- If you lie down with dogs, you'll...stink in the morning.
- Don't put off till tomorrow what...you put on to go to bed.
- Children should be seen and not...spanked or grounded.

An English teacher in Edmonton says to her student, "There are two words I will not allow in my class. One is 'gross' and the other is 'cool.'"

From the back of the room, little Jimmy calls out, "So, what are the words?"

nglish teacher notices a boy staring out of the window and calls out a question, "You, boy! Quick, give me two pronouns."

The boy looks around and says, "Who? Me?"

A teacher is trying to explain addition to a young boy.

"Peter, if I laid two eggs over there and two eggs over here, how many would I have?"

"I don't know," says Peter. "Let's see you do it, first."

Father: "How do you like going to school?"

Son: "The going part and the coming part are fine, but I don't like the time in between."

Teacher: "Can someone tell me what happens to a car when it gets old and rusts?"

Mary: "My dad buys it."

Teacher: "Can you name an animal that lives in Iceland?"

Amir: "A reindeer."

Teacher: "Good, now can you name another?"

Amir: "Another reindeer."

Teacher: "I asked you to draw sheep eating grass while I was out of the room. You've only drawn sheep."

Student: "You were out so long that the sheep ate all the grass."

A student has a single question on his final exam that asks, "What is courage?" The student writes the word "This" on the exam, signs it and hands it in.

Teacher: "I hope I didn't just see you looking at Jimmy's paper."

Student: "I hope you didn't see me, either!"

A little boy is called up to the teacher's desk after class. "This essay you've written about your pet dog is copied directly from your brother's essay."

"Of course," says the boy. "It's the same dog."

Teacher: "If 1+1=2, and 2+2=4, what is 4+4?"

Student: "That's not fair! You answered the easy ones and left us with the hard one!"

Teacher: "Thomas, this letter from your father looks like it was written by you."

Thomas: "That's just because he borrowed my pen."

Donald MacDonald from Scotland goes to study at McGill University and is living in the residence with all the other students studying there. After he has been there a month, his mother comes to visit him.

"And how do you find the Canadian students, Donald?" she asks.

"Mother," he replies, "they're such terrible, noisy people. The one on that side keeps banging his head on the wall and won't stop. The one on the other side screams and screams all night."

"Oh, Donald! How do you manage to put up with these awful, noisy Canadian neighbours?"

"Mother, I do nothing. I just ignore them. I just stay here quietly playing my bagpipes."

A young girl in class, when asked to draw a picture of the Holy Family, produces a picture in which Mary and the baby Jesus are sitting on a donkey, led by Joseph. On the ground nearby, the little girl has drawn a black blob.

"What is that?" asks the teacher.

"The flea," answers the young girl.

"What flea, dear?" asks the puzzled teacher.

"The one the angel told Joseph to take."

Eventually, puzzled, but not liking to challenge an imaginative child, the teacher checks out her Bible. And there it is: Matthew 2:13 "…the angel of the Lord saying, Arise, and take the young child and his mother, and flee into Egypt…"

I thought I saw an eye doctor on an Alaskan island, but it turned out to be an optical Aleutian.

Recently, a demonstration by a large number of students took place at several schools across Canada. The students were protesting the fact that the teachers get paid, when it was they who did all the work.

A science teacher is teaching his class about "observation." He takes out a jar of yellow-coloured liquid.

"This," he explains, "is urine. To be a doctor, you have to be observant to colour, smell, sight and taste."

After saying this, he dips his finger into the jar and puts it into his mouth. His class watches on in amazement, most in disgust. But, being the good students that they are, they pass the jar around. One by one, they dip one finger into the jar and then put it into their mouths.

After the last student is done, the teacher shakes his head and says, "If any of you had been observant, you would have noticed that I put my second finger into the jar and my third finger into my mouth."

## A History of Teaching Math

1.  Teaching math in the 1950s: A logger sells a truckload of lumber for $100. His cost of production is four-fifths of the price. What is his profit?

2.  Teaching math in the 1960s: A logger sells a truckload of lumber for $100. His cost of production is four-fifths of the price, or $80. What is his profit?

3.  Teaching math in the 1970s: A logger exchanges a set "L" of lumber for a set "M" of money. The cardinality of set "M" is 100. Each element is worth one dollar. Make 100 dots representing the elements of the set "M." The set "C," the cost of production, contains 20 fewer points than set "M." Represent the set "C" as a subset of set "M" and answer the following question: What is the cardinality of the set "P" of profits?

4.  Teaching math in the 1980s: A logger sells a truckload of lumber for $100. His cost of

production is $80, and his profit is $20. Your assignment: Underline the number 20.

5. Teaching math in the 1990s: By cutting down beautiful forest trees, the logger makes $20. What do you think of this way of making a living? Topic for class participation after answering the question: How did the forest birds and squirrels feel as the logger cut down the trees? There are no wrong answers.

6. Teaching math in the 2000s: Your call.

At Sunday school, the children are taught that God created everything, including human beings. Little Johnny, a child in the kindergarten class, seems especially intent when they tell him how Eve was created out of one of Adam's ribs.

The teacher confiscated a rubber band pistol during algebra class because it was a weapon of math disruption.

Later in the week, Johnny's mother notices him lying down as if he was ill, and asks, "Johnny, what's the matter?"

Little Johnny groans and responds, "I have a pain in my side. I think I'm going to have a wife."

Teacher: "You missed school yesterday, didn't you?"

Student: "Yes, but not very much."

A teacher notices that little Billy has been day-dreaming for a long time. She decides to get his attention.

"Billy," she says, "If the world is 25,000 miles around and eggs are 60 cents a dozen, how old am I?

"Thirty-four," replies Billy without hesitating.

The teacher replies, "Well, that's not far from my actual age. Tell me...how did you guess?"

Q: Why were the teacher's eyes crossed?

A: She couldn't control her pupils.

"Oh, there's nothing to it," says Billy. "My big sister is 17, and she's only half crazy."

A little girl is diligently pounding away on her father's laptop. She tells him she is writing a story.

"What's it about?" he asks.

"I don't know," replies the little girl. "I can't read."

Teacher: "Name two days of the week that start with "T."

Student: "Today and Tomorrow."

Teacher: "Could you please pay a little attention?"

Student: "I'm paying as little attention as I can."

Little Randy has finished his summer vacation and is back at school. Two days later, his teacher phones Randy's mother to tell her that Randy has been misbehaving.

"Wait a minute," says Randy's mother. "I had Randy with me for three months and I never called you once when he misbehaved."

Teacher: "Why are you late for school?"

Student: "Because of the sign."

Teacher: "What sign?"

Student: "The sign that says, 'School Ahead, Go Slow.'"

While visiting a country school, the chairman of the Board of Education becomes provoked at the noise the unruly students are making in the next room. Angrily, he opens the door and grabs one of the taller boys who seems to be doing most of the talking. The chairman takes the boy to the next room and makes him stand in the corner. A few minutes later, a small boy sticks his head in the room and pleads, "Please, sir, may we have our teacher back?"

A teacher arrives late for class to find a most uncomplimentary drawing of himself on the blackboard. Fuming, he asks the class joker in the front row, "Who is responsible for this?"

The joker wins tremendous prestige with his reply, "I really don't know, but I strongly suspect its parents."

Finding one of her students making faces at others on the playground, Ms. Smith gently reproves the child. Smiling sweetly, she says, "Bobby, when I was a child, I was told that if I made an ugly face, it would freeze and I would stay like that."

Bobby looks up and replies, "Well, Ms. Smith, you can't say you weren't warned."

## CHAPTER TWO

# What Did You Just Say?

Little girl: "Daddy, Daddy, can I have another glass of water please?"

Father: "But I've given you 10 glasses of water already!"

Little girl: "Yes, but the bedroom is still on fire!"

A duck walks into a newspaper's classified offices, takes out a blank form and writes, "Quack, Quack, Quack, Quack, Quack, Quack."

The clerk on duty studies the form and says, "There are only six words here. You can have another 'Quack' for the same price."

The duck replies, "Now that would just be silly."

## Mall Santa

A mother takes her spoiled young son to the mall to meet Santa Claus.

"What would you like for Christmas, young man?" asks Santa with a deep belly laugh.

"I want a PlayStation, a new bike and a new baseball glove," replies the boy.

"I will do my best, young man, to see that you get what your heart desires," says Santa.

Later in the day, the mother takes her son to another mall, and once again they visit Santa.

"What would you like for Christmas, young man?" asks the jolly mall Santa.

"A PlayStation, a new bike and a new baseball glove," says the spoiled little boy.

"And are you going to be a good boy, help your mother and do your homework?" asks Santa.

The boy turns to his mother and says, "Let's go back to the first mall. I didn't have to make promises with that Santa."

Q: What do you call cheese that isn't yours?

A: Nacho cheese.

Timothy is sitting calmly in the dentist's chair while having his teeth worked on when suddenly the dentist stops and says, "Would you mind letting out a piercing scream?"

"Why? It doesn't hurt at all," says Timothy.

"I know, but I have a waiting room full of patients, and the hockey game starts in an hour."

A man goes into a bookstore and asks the saleswoman, "Where's the self-help section?"

The woman replies, "If I tell you, it would defeat the purpose."

## Cannibals

Three men become lost in the jungle and are captured by cannibals. The cannibal king tells the men they can live if they undertake a trial.

"The first step of the trial is that each of you must go into the forest and find 10 pieces of the same fruit," says the king. The men go into the forest and soon the first man comes back with 10 apples.

Q:  What flower grows on your face?

A:  Tulips.

The king then explains the trial: "Now you must take the fruit and insert it into your bum without any expression on your face. If you make a sound or move a muscle on your face, you will be eaten."

The first man puts one apple in his bum, but on the second apple, he grimaces and is eaten by the cannibals.

The second man returns from the forest with 10 berries. He inserts the first nine berries without making a sound, but on the tenth berry, he suddenly bursts out laughing and is eaten up by the cannibals.

The two dead men meet up in heaven. The first man says to the second man, "Why did you laugh on the final berry? You were almost free."

"I know," replies the second man, "but I saw the third guy coming out of the forest with an armful of pineapples!"

Three kids go to their friend's house to swim in his pool. Their friend tells them that the pool is magical, and that when they each jump off the diving board, they will land in anything they want to.

So, the three kids go over to the diving board. The first kid, a vegetarian, jumps off the diving board and yells out, "BANANAS!" and lands in a pool of bananas.

Q: Why can't you go to the bathroom at a Beatles reunion?
A: There's no John.

The second kid is money hungry and yells out, "MONEY!" and lands in a pile of money.

The third kid jumps off the diving board, and just then a bird poops on his head. He yells, "OH CRAP!"

A burglar breaks into a house. He sees a CD player that he wants, so he takes it. Then he hears a voice: "Jesus is watching you." The burglar looks around with his flashlight, wondering "What the heck was that?" He then spots some money on a table and takes it.

Once again he hears a voice: "Jesus is ⌐. you." The burglar hides in a corner, trying to fig⌐ out where the voice is coming from. He sees a bird-cage with a parrot in it. He goes over and asks, "Was that your voice?"

The parrot says, "Yes."

"What's your name?" asks the burglar.

The parrot says, "Moses."

"What kind of person names his bird 'Moses'?" asks the burglar.

The parrot replies, "The same person who names his rottweiler 'Jesus.'"

Lance walks past a mental hospital and hears a cackling voice: "13...13...13...13." Lance looks over to the hospital and sees a hole in the wall. He looks through the hole and gets poked in the eye. The voice then says, "14...14...14...14."

An elderly man is walking down a country road in Saskatchewan and sees a young farmer struggling to load hay back onto a cart after it has fallen off. "You look hot, my son," says the old man. "Why don't you rest a moment, and I'll give you a hand."

"No, thanks," replies the young man. "My father won't like it."

"Don't be silly," the old man says. "Everyone is entitled to a break. Come and have a drink of water."

Again the young man protests that his father will be upset.

No matter how much you push the envelope, it'll still be stationery.

Losing his patience, the old man says, "Your father must be a real slave driver. Tell me where I can find him, and I'll give him a piece of my mind!"

"Well," replies the young farmer, "he's under the load of hay."

A mother and her young son return home from the grocery store and begin putting away the groceries. The boy opens a box of animal crackers and spreads the crackers all over the table.

"What are you doing?" asks his mother.

"The box says you can't eat them if the seal is broken," the boy explains, "so I'm looking for the seal!"

A salesman walking down the street in Winnipeg sees a young boy sitting on a porch and says, "Hi there, sonny. Is your mommy at home?"

"She sure is," replies the boy.

The salesman rings the bell, then again and again, but gets no answer. He turns to the boy and says, "Hey, I thought you said your mommy was at home."

"She is," replies the boy. "But I don't live here."

One day, while they are out shopping, a little boy embarrasses his mother by loudly saying he needs to pee.

His mother tells him, "Don't shout out like that. In the future, if you need to pee, just say 'I want a whisper,' and I'll know what you mean."

A few days later, the boy goes into his parents' bedroom and finds his dad having a nap. "What do you want, son?" asks the dad.

"I want a whisper," says the little boy.

"Okay," replies the dad. "Whisper in my ear."

For several weeks, six-year-old Tommy has told his first-grade teacher about the baby brother or sister that is expected at his house.

> Q: What do you call a guy who hangs out with musicians?
>
> A: A drummer.

One day, Tommy's mother allows him to feel the movements of the unborn child. Tommy is obviously impressed, but he makes no comment. Furthermore, he stops telling his teacher about the impending event. The teacher finally says to him, "Tommy, whatever has become of that baby brother or sister you were expecting at home?"

Tommy bursts into tears and confesses, "I think Mommy ate it!"

Little Johnny's neighbours have just had a baby. Unfortunately, the little baby was born with no ears. When the new family arrives home from the hospital, the parents invite Johnny's family to come over and see their new baby. Little Johnny's parents are afraid that their son will have some wisecrack to say about the baby, so the dad has a long talk with little Johnny before going to the neighbours' house.

A dog gave birth to puppies near the road and was cited for littering.

The father says, "Now, son...that poor baby was born without any ears. I want you to be on your best behaviour and not say one word about his ears, or I am really going to spank you when we get back home."

"I promise not to mention his ears at all," says Johnny.

At the neighbour's home, little Johnny leans over in the crib and touches the baby's hand.

He looks at the baby's mother and says, "Oh, what a beautiful little baby!"

The mother smiles and says, "Thank you very much, Johnny."

Johnny then says, "This baby has perfect little hands and perfect little feet. Why...just look at his pretty little eyes. Did his doctor say that he can see good?"

The mother relies, "Why, yes, Johnny. The doctor said he has 20/20 vision."

> A grenade thrown into a kitchen in France would result in Linoleum Blownapart.

Little Johnny replies, "Well, it's a darn good thing, 'cause he sure couldn't wear glasses!"

A little boy opens the Bible with fascination and looks at the old pages as he turns them. Suddenly, something falls out of the Bible, and he picks it up and gazes at it closely. It's a dried leaf that has been pressed in between the pages.

"Momma, look what I found!" the boy calls out.

"What have you got there, dear?" his mother asks.

With astonishment in the young boy's voice, he answers, "I think it's Adam's suit!"

Little Susie is Mommy's helper. She helps set the table when company is coming for dinner. Soon, everything is on the table. Mr. Smythe, their guest, arrives, and everyone sits down at the table to eat.

The mother notices something is missing.

"Susie, dear," she says, "you didn't put a knife and fork at Mr. Smythe's place."

"But, Mommy, I thought he wouldn't need them," explains Susie. "Daddy says he always eats like a horse."

CHAPTER THREE

# The World of the Imagination

## New Career

An out-of-work ventriloquist decides it's time to find a new career. While looking through the classifieds section in the newspaper, he sees an ad for a fortunetelling business. He decides to buy the business and become a fortune teller. He posts a price list in the window of his home and waits for his first customer.

Before long, his first customer walks in and asks about the prices.

"I have three prices," says the ventriloquist. "For $20, you will hear a sound made by your dearly departed. For $30, you will hear the voice of your lost loved one."

"What can I get for $50?" asks the customer.

"For $50," replies the ventriloquist, "you'll hear the voice of the dearly departed...while I drink a glass of water."

"You must meet my friend. She's a medium," says a woman to her friend.

"No, it'll only depress me," replies the friend. "I'm a large."

Astronaut #1: "How do you hold up your space pants?"

Astronaut #2: "I wear an asteroid belt."

Three vampires sit down at a table in a restaurant and order their favourite drinks.

One vampire says, "I vant some blood!"

The second vampire says, "I vant some blood, too!"

The third vampire says, "Just plasma for me, please."

The waitress takes the order, then walks over to the counter and yells, "Give me two bloods and a blood lite!"

Q: What do you call a dog owned by Dracula?

A: A blood hound.

Q: Why did King Kong join the army?

A: To learn about gorilla warfare.

A Canadian ghost goes on vacation to Italy to scare people. He tries and tries to scare people, but he can't seem to get any reactions. Finally, he meets an Italian ghost.

"How do I have more fun and scare people here?" asks the Canadian ghost.

The Italian ghost replies, "When in Rome, boo as the Romans boo."

Jason is walking down the street when he sees a man who has an orange for a head.

"What happened to you?" asks Jason.

"I released a genie from a magic lamp, and it gave me three wishes. My first wish was to be incredibly rich, and my second wish was that I would be the strongest man in the world."

"Okay," says Jason. "What was your third wish?"

"Isn't it obvious? I wished I had an orange for a head."

A teenager is walking along a beach when he comes across a lamp. He picks it up, rubs it, and a genie pops out. In exchange for freeing him, the genie offers the teenager three wishes.

"I'd like to have 10 million dollars." Poof! The money appears at the boy's feet.

"I'd like a new Ferrari," says the teenager. Poof! A new red Ferrari appears in front of him.

Finally the teenager says, "I want to be irresistible to all girls." Poof! He turns into a box of chocolates.

Q: What do you get if you deep fry Santa Claus?

A: Crisp Cringle.

Q: What nationality is Santa Claus?

A: North Polish.

The year you stop believing in Santa Claus is the year you start getting clothes for gifts.

Little Red Riding Hood is walking through the forest when she sees a wolf hiding behind a bush. Playfully, she slips up behind him and taps him on the shoulder.

"My, what big eyes you have!" she says.

The wolf runs off and hides behind another bush. Little Red Riding Hood follows him and taps him on the shoulder again.

"My, what a big nose you have!" she says.

The wolf screams and runs off behind another bush. Little Red Riding Hood sneaks up on him again and again taps him on the shoulder.

If you jumped off the bridge in Paris, you'd be in Seine.

"My, what big teeth you have!" she says.

The wolf turns on her and shouts, "DO YOU MIND! I'm trying to go to the bathroom!"

Ad in a newspaper: Telepath wanted. You know where to apply.

A woman comes home from a psychic fair with a crystal ball she's just bought.

"How much was that?" asks her husband.

"Fifty dollars," answers the woman.

"Fifty!" says the husband. "They must have seen you coming."

Tom takes a shortcut through a graveyard at midnight and is disturbed to hear a regular tapping sound. The noise gets louder, and Tom stumbles across a man in a suit tapping away at a headstone with a chisel. Tom looks over the man's shoulder and sees that the man is adding an "e" to the end of the name carved in the stone.

"A little late for work like that, isn't it?" says Tom.

Q: Did you hear about the giant who threw up?

A: It's all over town.

"Yes," says the man. "But it couldn't wait. They spelled my name wrong."

Tom runs for his life.

Three little pigs go out to dinner one night. The waiter comes and takes their drink order. "I would like a Sprite," says the first little piggie.

"I would like a Coke," says the second little piggie.

ant water, lots and lots of water," says the third little piggie.

The drinks are brought out, and the waiter takes their orders for dinner.

"I want a nice big steak," says the first piggie.

"I would like the salad plate," says the second piggie.

"I want water, lots and lots of water," says the third little piggie. The meals are brought out, and a while later, the waiter approaches the table and asks if the piggies would like any dessert.

"I want a banana split," says the first piggie.

"I want a root beer float," says the second piggie.

"I want water, lots and lots of water," exclaims the third little piggie.

"Pardon me for asking," says the waiter, "but why have you only ordered water?"

The third piggie says, "Well, somebody has to go 'Wee, wee, wee' all the way home!"

Q: What do you get if you cross King Kong with a budgie?

A: A messy cage.

## The Three Stages of Life

1) You believe in Santa Claus.

2) You don't believe in Santa Claus.

3) You are Santa Claus.

## CHAPTER FOUR

# Grownups Are Weird

A man with a nagging secret couldn't keep it in any longer. In the confessional at church, he admits that for years he has been stealing building supplies from the lumberyard where he works.

"What did you take?" his priest asks.

"Enough to build my own house and enough for my son's house, as well as houses for my two daughters and our cottage at the lake."

"This is very serious," the priest says. "I shall have to think of a far-reaching penance. Have you ever done a retreat?"

"No, Father, I haven't," the man replies. "But if you can get the plans, I can get the lumber."

A man walks into the doctor's office with a zucchini in his left ear, a carrot in his right ear and a cucumber up his nose.

"What's wrong with me, doc?" asks the man.

---

Q: What do monsters make with cars?

A: Traffic jam.

"It's a simple diagnosis," replies the doctor. "You're not eating properly."

A woman goes to a lawyer to ask some questions about getting a divorce.

"What grounds do you have, madam?"

"About six acres."

"No, I don't think you understand. Let me say again. Do you have a grudge?"

"No, just a parking space."

"I'll try again," says the lawyer. "Does your husband beat you up?"

"No, I always get up an hour before he does," she answers.

Almost giving up on the woman, the lawyer asks one final question, "Are you sure you want to get divorced?"

"Yes, my husband doesn't understand anything I say!"

Two guys are roaring down a country road on a motorcycle when the driver slows down and pulls over. His leather jacket has a broken zipper, and he tells his friend, "I can't drive anymore with the air hitting me in the chest like that."

"Just put the jacket on backwards," advises his friend.

The driver puts his jacket on backwards, and they continue down the road. Going around the next bend, they lose control of the motorcycle and wipe out. A man comes upon the accident and calls the police on his cell phone.

"Are they showing any signs of life?" asks the police officer on the phone.

"Well," explains the man, "the driver was, until I turned his head the right way around!"

Three construction workers are eating lunch one day.

The first one opens his lunchbox and says, "Eeew, turkey! I hate turkey!" So he shoots himself with a rivet gun.

The second one opens his lunchbox and says, "Eeew, ham! I hate ham!" So he jumps off the building.

The third one opens his box and says, "Eeew, mac and cheese! I hate mac and cheese!" So he runs himself over with a bulldozer.

At the funeral, the wives of the three men are talking about their lost husbands. The first two are very sad, but the third is rather puzzled.

The first wife says, "I thought he liked turkey!"

The second one says, "I thought he liked ham!"

But the third one is still puzzled. She says, "I thought he packed his own lunch."

One evening, a little girl and her parents are sitting around the table eating supper. The little girl says, "Daddy, you're the boss, aren't you?"

The girl's daddy smiles, pleased, and says, "Yes."

The little girl says, "That's because Mommy put you in charge, right?"

A man walks into a shoe store and tries on a pair of shoes.

"How do they feel?" asks the sales clerk.

"Well, they feel a bit tight," replies the man.

The assistant bends down and has a look at the shoes and the man's feet.

"Try pulling the tongue out," suggests the clerk.

"Nath, theyth sthill feelth a bith tighth," he says.

One day a little girl is watching her mother do the dishes at the kitchen sink. She suddenly notices that her mother has several strands of white hair sticking out in contrast to her brunette head.

She looks at her mother and asks, "Why are some of your hairs white, Mom?"

Her mother replies, "Well, every time you do something wrong and make me cry or unhappy, one of my hairs turns white."

The little girl thinks about this revelation for a while and then asks, "Momma, how come ALL of grandma's hairs are white?"

A man goes to see his doctor. The doctor asks what is wrong, and the man says, "Doctor, I think I'm a moth."

To this the doctor responds, "You think you're a moth? Well, I don't think you need a doctor. It sounds like what you really need is a therapist."

"Yeah, I know," replies the patient. "I was on my way to see a therapist, but I came in here because I saw your light was on."

> Q: What do you get if you cross King Kong with a giant frog?
>
> A: A monster that climbs up the Empire State Building and catches airplanes with its tongue.

Every Saturday morning, Grandpa Walt finds himself babysitting his three grandchildren, all boys. The kids always want to play "War," and Grandpa always gets coaxed into the game.

One Saturday, his daughter comes home to pick up the kids early and sees Grandpa take a fake shot as one of the boys points a toy gun at him and yells, "Bang!"

Grandpa slumps to the floor and stays there, motionless. The daughter rushes over to see if he is all right. Grandpa opens one eye and whispers, "Shhh, I always do this. It's the only chance I get to rest."

A woman's husband has been slipping in and out of a coma for several months, yet she has stayed by his bedside every single day. One day, he comes to and motions for her to move closer. As she sits by him, he whispers, eyes full of tears, "You know what? You have been with me through all the bad times. When I got fired, you were there to support me. When my business failed, you were there. When I got shot, you were by my side. When we lost the house, you stayed right here. When my health started failing, you were still by my side. You know what?"

"What dear?" she asks gently, smiling as her heart begins to fill with warmth.

"I think you're bad luck!"

Jimmy's mom drags him in front of his dad during a football game.

"Talk to your son," she says. "He refuses to listen to a word I say."

The father turns to Jimmy angrily. "Jimmy, how dare you disobey your mother. Do you think you're better than your old man?"

Two blondes are leaving a store. One of the blondes owns a Mustang and has locked her keys in the car. She tries to pick the lock when she stops to rest for a second.

As she sits down, her friend says, "Hurry up, it's starting to rain, and the top's down!"

James leaves a note on his office door saying, "Back in an hour."

When he gets back from lunch, he sees the sign and so he sits down and waits.

A teacher gives her fifth- grade class an assignment: Get their parents to tell them a story with a moral at the end of it. The next day, the kids begin to tell their stories.

Kathy says, "My father's a farmer, and we have a lot of egg-laying hens. One time we were taking our eggs to market in a basket on

Q: What do you say when you meet a two-headed monster?

A: Hello! Hello!

the front seat of the pickup when we hit a bump in the road, and all the eggs went flying and broke and made a mess."

"And what's the moral of the story?" asks the teacher.

"Don't put all your eggs in one basket!"

"Very good," says the teacher.

Next, little Lucy raises her hand and says, "Our family are farmers, too. But we raise chickens for the meat market. We had a dozen eggs one time, but when they hatched, we only got 10 live chicks, and the moral to this story is, don't count your chickens before they hatch."

"That was a fine story, Lucy. Jessie, do you have a story to share?"

"Yes, ma'am! My daddy told me this story about my Aunt Marge. She was a flight engineer during Desert Storm and her plane got hit. She had to bail out over enemy territory, and all she had was a machine gun and a machete. She landed right in the middle of 100 enemy troops. She killed 70 of them with the machine gun until it ran out of bullets! Then she killed 20 more with the machete till the blade broke. Then she killed the last 10 with her bare hands."

"Good heavens," says the horrified teacher, "what kind of moral did your daddy tell you from that horrible story?"

"Stay away from Aunt Marge when she's angry!"

Little Joey's kindergarten class is on a field trip to their local police station. They see pictures of the 10 most wanted criminals tacked to a bulletin board. One of the youngsters points to a picture and asks if it really is the photo of a wanted person.

"Yes," replies the police officer. "The detectives want very badly to capture him."

Little Joey asks, "Why didn't you keep him when you took his picture?"

Tom has a problem getting up in the morning, and he is always late for work. His boss is angry at him and threatens to fire him if he doesn't do something about it. So, Tom goes to his doctor, who gives him a pill and tells him to take it before he goes to sleep. Tom sleeps well that night, and in fact, he wakes up before the alarm in the morning. He has a leisurely breakfast and then drives cheerfully to work.

"Boss," he says, "the pill actually worked!"

"That's all fine," replies the boss, "but where were you yesterday?"

In the hustle and bustle of holiday shopping, a woman drops her purse. An honest little boy notices her drop the purse, so he picks it up and returns it to her. The woman looks into her purse and comments, "Hmm.... That's funny. When

I lost my purse, there was a 20-dollar bill in it. Now there are 20 loonies."

The boy quickly replies, "That's right, lady. The last time I found a purse, the owner didn't have any change for a reward."

The privilege of naming all the children of a tribe always falls to the chief. One day, a small Native boy asks the chief how he chose the names for all the children.

"Well, my son," the chief replies, "when I step out of my teepee, I name each child after the first thing I see. For instance, when a child is born and I step out of my teepee and see a pale moon rising, I say, 'You shall be called, Pale Moon Rising.'"

> Q: What do you get if King Kong sits on your piano?
>
> A: A flat note.

"And when a child is born and I step out of my teepee and see a hawk flying over, I say, "You shall be called, Hawk Flying Over."

"So why do you ask, Big Dog Pooping?"

A little girl runs up to her mother and asks, "Mommy, where do babies comes from?"

"The stork, dear," replies the mother.

"Mommy, who keeps bad people from robbing the house?" asks the girl.

"The police, dear," says the mother.

"Mommy, if the house was on fire, who would save us?"

"The firemen, dear."

Two silk worms had a race. They ended up in a tie.

"Mommy, where does food come from?" asks the little girl.

"Farmers, dear," answers the mother.

"Mommy," says the girl, "then what do we need Daddy for?"

Dick and Tom find three hand grenades in a field and decide to take them to the police station. "But what if one of them blows up?" asks Dick.

"Well, in that case, we'll just tell them we found two," says Tom.

A man asks his wife, "What would you most like for your birthday?"

She replies, "I'd love to be 10 again."

On the morning of her birthday, the husband wakes up his wife bright and early, and off they go to a theme park. He puts her on every ride in the park: the Death Slide, the Screaming Loop, the Wall of Fear. Every ride there was, she went on it.

Five hours later, the wife staggers out of the theme park, her head reeling and her stomach upside down. The couple goes to McDonald's, where her husband orders her a Double Big Mac with extra fries and a strawberry shake. Then they go to a movie theatre and have more burgers, popcorn, cola and sweets. At last, she staggers home with her husband and collapses into bed.

Her husband leans over and asks, "Well, dear, what was it like being 10 again?"

She opens one eye, groans and says, "Actually, I meant dress size."

A woman holding a baby in her arms gets on a bus. The bus driver says, "That's the ugliest baby I've ever seen."

In a huff, the woman slams her fare into the fare box and sits down in an aisle seat near the rear of the bus. The man seated next to her senses that she is agitated and asks her what is wrong.

"The bus driver insulted me!" she fumes.

The man sympathizes and says, "Why, he's a public servant and shouldn't say things to insult passengers."

"You're right," she replies. "I think I'll go back up there and give him a piece of my mind."

"That's a good idea," says the man. "Here, let me hold your monkey."

A man has been driving all night along the highway and decides to stop in the next town early in the morning to get a few hours of sleep. As his bad luck would have it, he pulls into a park full of joggers. Just as he is about to drift off into dreamland, a jogger spots the man and starts knocking on the window. "Excuse me, sir," says the jogger. "Do you have the time?"

The man looks at his car clock and says, "It's 7:30 AM."

The jogger thanks him and runs on his way.

Ten minutes later, as the man is just about to fall asleep again, another jogger comes running by and begins knocking on the window.

"Excuse me, sir, do you have the time?" asks the jogger.

"It's 7:40 AM!" snaps the man.

To prevent any more interruptions, the man writes a note that says, "I do not know the time!" He posts the note on his window for all the joggers to see. He then settles back into his seat, ready to get some shut-eye.

A few minutes later, another jogger taps on his window and says, "Excuse me, sir. It's 7:55 AM."

## CHAPTER FIVE

# Sports Jokes

## Toronto Maple Leaf Hunters

A group of Toronto Maple Leaf players go on a hunting trip and set up camp deep in the woods.

That evening, one of the men walks into the camp, and with an uneasy look on his face, asks, "Is everybody here?"

One of the men says, "Yes."

The exasperated hunter asks, "Nobody's hurt?"

"No."

"Thank God!" says the hunter. "That means I just shot a deer!"

## Hotline

The Nashville Predators have apparently set up a call centre for fans who are troubled by their current form. The number is 1-800-10-10-10. Calls are charged at peak rate for overseas users. Once again, that number is 1-800-won-nothing-won-nothing-won-nothing.

## Three Wishes

A man is strolling along a riverside park in Chicago when he spots a bottle floating in the water.

The bottle drifts ashore. He picks up the bottle and opens it. Out pops a genie.

Q: How many Canadians does it take to screw in a light bulb?

A: No one knows. They are all too busy playing hockey to care about some stupid light bulb.

"Master, you have released me from my bondage in this bottle. Ask any three wishes and I will grant them to you."

The man thinks for a moment and says, "I would like three things to happen this year: the Toronto Blue Jays win the World Series, the Toronto Raptors win the NBA title, and the Toronto Maple Leafs win the Stanley Cup."

The genie thinks about this for a moment...and jumps back into the bottle.

## Season Tickets

Darlene is watching television in the living room with her husband, who is quietly reading a book.

"Sweetheart," she says. "Did you hear the story of the guy from Long Island who swapped his wife for a season pass to the Islanders games? Would you give me up for something like that?"

"Now why would I go and do a stupid thing like that?" he replies. "The season's half over."

## I Smart

A half an hour before football practice, a player walks into the medical room and says, "Doc, I hurt all over."

Even though it's the doctor's first day on the job, he is not naïve enough to believe the player, so he says, "That's impossible. You're just trying to get the day off, right?"

"No, really, I hurt all over," the player insists. "Look. When I touch my arm, ouch. When I touch my leg, ouch. When I touch my chest, ouch. When I touch my head, ouch."

The doctor just nods and asks, "You've had more than 10 concussions, haven't you?"

The player looks puzzled and then says, "Yes, but how do you know?"

The doctor replies, "Because your finger is broken."

## Doctor!

After only a few games playing for the Montreal Canadiens, the new goaltender has already let in 10 goals. He is eating supper in a restaurant one evening when a man approaches him and says, "I've been watching you play, and I think I might be able to help you."

"Are you a trainer?" says the dejected Canadiens goalkeeper.

"No," replies the stranger, "I'm an optician."

## The Wife's Lesson

Jimmy's wife constantly nags him to teach her to play golf. Finally, one morning he relents and he takes her to the club. On the first hole, a 179-yards par-3, he tees up first and says, "Now watch me, and do the same thing."

In Canada we have two seasons: six months of winter and six months of poor hockey weather.

He hits a nice shot and lands on the green, 30 feet from the cup.

His wife steps up, drills it, hooks it and bounces it off a rock, clips a tree, sideswipes a second rock. The ball rolls up onto the green and goes in.

The husband looks at her in shock and says, "Okay, now you know how to play. Let's go home."

## Demons

The Devil is holding a meeting with all the new demons. He stands up and says, "Well, you poor, useless lot of sissies, there is too much good in the world. You are all time wasters, and you make me sick. You came to hell to help make man's life a misery. Instead, you're wasting time playing silly games. So what are you going to do about it?"

Just then, a small devil who is quite new to the job and very timid, sheepishly says, "Oh, Lord of great darkness, I know I'm not as powerful as you, but may I make a suggestion? It seems to me that if we could build them up and knock them down, the pain would be so great that we would soon gain control."

Just as he says this, a more experienced demon says, "You mean golf?"

The Devil interrupts, saying, "Steady on, old man, we don't want to finish them off that quick!"

## Religious Battle Golf

The Pope is meeting with the College of Cardinals to discuss a proposal from Shimon Peres, the former leader of Israel.

"Your Holiness," says one of the cardinals, "Mr. Peres wants to determine whether Jews or Catholics are superior, by challenging you to a golf match."

The Pope is greatly disturbed, as he has never held a golf club in his life.

Q: Did you hear the one about the overweight ballerina?

A: She had to wear a three-three.

"Not to worry," says the cardinal. "We'll call America and talk to Jack Nicklaus. We'll make him a cardinal; he can play Shimon Peres. We can't lose!"

Everyone agrees it's a good idea. The call is made and, of course, Jack is honoured and agrees to play.

The day after the match, Nicklaus reports to the Vatican and informs the Pope of his success in the match.

"I came in second, your Holiness," says Nicklaus.

"Second?!" exclaims the Pope in great surprise. "You came in second to Shimon Peres?!"

"No," replies Nicklaus, "second to Rabbi Woods."

*Canadian hockey has been carried to all parts of the world, usually on a stretcher.*

–Eric Nichol and Dave More
in their 1978 book, *The Joy of Hockey*

*Canadians can't play baseball because baseball is a summer game, and Canada has no summer. Canadians should stick to their native sports, namely, hockey and pelt trapping.*

–Jimmy Breslin , American writer, commenting on singer Mary O'Dowd's forgetting the words to the U.S. national anthem at a Toronto Blue Jays–New York Yankees game

Four out of five dentists surveyed recommend playing hockey.

Teacher: "Aaron, would you stand up in front of the class and name the four seasons of the year?"

Aaron: "No problem, teacher. Hockey, basketball, baseball and vacation."

## At the Hockey Game

Mom: "Was there a fight at the game today? You've lost your front teeth."

Son: "No, I haven't. They're in my pocket."

## The Greatest One

A young hockey-loving kid dies and goes to heaven, where he meets St. Peter at the Pearly Gates.

"Do you want to join the Good Guys in heaven," asks St. Peter, "or the Bad Guys?"

"The Good Guys, of course," says the kid.

St. Peter shows him the way. Just then, one of the Good Guys appears, pushing everybody out of the way, stickhandling a puck through the crowd.

"If that bully is one of the Good Guys, what are the Bad Guys like?" asks the kid.

"I know what you're thinking," answers St. Peter. "But that's not a Bad Guy. That's only God; sometimes he likes to pretend he's Wayne Gretzky."

Panting and perspiring, two men on a tandem bicycle at last get to the top of a steep hill.

"That was a stiff climb," says the first man.

"It certainly was," replies the second man. "And if I hadn't kept the brake on, we would have slid down backward!"

Hockey players have been complaining about violence for years. It's just that without any teeth, no one can understand them.

Little Timmy arrives home after his soccer game, throws open the door and runs to his dad.

"How was the game, son? How did you do?" asks his father, who was unable to attend the game.

"You aren't going to believe it, Dad!" exclaims Timmy. "I was responsible for the winning goal!"

"That's wonderful," replies his dad. "How did you do that?"

"I missed my check on the other team's high scorer!"

## Hockey Night in Canada?

Play-by-play announcer in a game between the Vancouver Canucks and the Toronto Maple Leafs: "And here comes the Leafs' Grabovski, with a pass to Antropov, then it's to Kulemin. Oh, the Canucks Hordichuk grabs the puck, then shoots a quick pass to Demitra, over to Bieska, to the point to Ohlund. The block, it's picked up by the Leafs, and here comes Blake...Blake? What kind of ridiculous name is Blake for a hockey player?"

## Mammals vs. Insects

A team of mammals is playing a team of insects. The mammals totally dominate during the first half of the hockey game and at halftime are leading 28–0. However, at halftime, the insects make a substitution and bring on a centipede. The centipede scores an incredible 200 goals in the second half, and the insects win the game by a final score of 200–28. In the dressing room after the game, the captain of the mammals is chatting to the captain of the insects.

> Q: Why do so many Polish names end in "ski"?
>
> A: Because they can't spell "toboggan."

"That centipede of yours is terrific," says the mammal's captain. "Why didn't you play him from the start?"

"We would have liked to," replies the insect captain, "but it takes him 45 minutes to get his skates on."

## Soccer Knowledge

Patricia is beginning her job as a school counsellor and is keen to help the students. One day during recess, she notices a girl standing all by herself on one side of the playing field while the rest of the children are enjoying a game of soccer at the other end of the field. Patricia goes up to the girl and asks if she is all right. The girl says that she is fine. Some time later, however, Patricia notices that the girl is in exactly the same spot, still by herself.

Going up to her again, the school counsellor asks, "Would you like me to be your friend?"

The girl hesitates, then says, "Alright," while looking at Patricia suspiciously.

Feeling she is making some progress, Patricia asks, "Why are you standing here all alone?"

"Because," the girl says with a large sigh, "I'm the goalie!"

U.S. Olympian Peekaboo Street apparently came into a lot of money because of her Olympic performance. Rather than spend the money on herself, she showed a lot of character by donating it to a local hospital. The primary facility the hospital needed was a retrofit of the Intensive Care Unit, so in her honour, the hospital board is going to name the new unit "Peekaboo I.C.U."

Q:  Why did the captain lose the yacht race?

A:  He found himself in a no-wind situation.

One day, the Devil challenges God to a baseball game. Smiling, God proclaims, "You don't have a chance. I have Babe Ruth, Mickey Mantle and all the greatest players up here."

"Yes," snickers the Devil, "but I have all the umpires."

One day, Satan is out for a walk through hell, making sure things are running smoothly. When he gets to the Lake of Fire, he sees a man sitting by the lake, relaxing in a lawn chair and not sweating or looking uncomfortable at all. Perplexed, Satan approaches him and says, "Young man, are you not hot or bothered by this heat?"

The man replies, "Oh no, not at all. I lived in downtown Toronto, and this weather is just like a typical July day in the city."

> Q: What can you serve that you cannot eat?
> A: A tennis ball.

Satan thinks that this is not a good sign, so he rushes back to his office and turns up the heat in hell another 100 degrees. Satisfied with himself, he again returns to the Lake of Fire to check on the young man. When he gets there, the man is showing a few beads of sweat, but that is all. Again Satan asks the Torontonian, "Are you hot and uncomfortable yet?"

The young man looks up and says, "No, the temperature is just like a hot August day in Toronto. I'm coping with it just fine."

Satan decides that he has to do something drastic to make this man's stay in hell unpleasant. He goes back to his office, turns the heat all the way down, then turns up the air conditioning. The temperature in hell quickly drops well below zero. As he approaches the Lake of Fire, Satan notices that it is now frozen over. He also sees the Torontonian jumping up and down wildly, waving his arms and yelling into the air.

Q:  Why did the football team go to the phone booth?

A:  To get their quarter back.

"This looks promising!" thinks Satan.

Coming closer, he finally makes out what the man is shouting: "The Leafs have won the Stanley Cup! The Leafs have won the Stanley Cup!"

The other day was Take Your Daughter to Work Day. The Toronto Maple Leafs had a fun time, playing a little pick-up game against their daughters. Unfortunately, the Leafs lost, 15–3.

A health teacher has just finished a lecture on mental health and proceeds to give an oral quiz to the class. Speaking specifically about depression, the teacher asks, "How would you diagnose a person who walks back and forth screaming at the top of his lungs one minute, then sits down weeping uncontrollably the next?"

A young student sitting in the rear of the classroom raises his hand and says, "A hockey dad?"

It's a cold winter day. An old man walks out onto a frozen lake, cuts a hole in the ice, drops in his fishing line and waits patiently for a bite. He is there for almost an hour, without even a nibble when a young boy walks out onto the lake and cuts a hole in the ice next to the old man. The young boy drops his fishing line, and minutes later, he hooks a largemouth bass. The old man can't believe his eyes but chalks it up to plain luck. Shortly thereafter, the young boy pulls in another large catch. The young boy keeps catching fish after fish.

> Q: How do you know a leper is playing ice hockey?
>
> A: There's a "face-off"' in the corner.

Finally, the old man can't take it any longer. "Son," he says, "I've been here for over an hour without even a nibble. You've been here only a few minutes and have caught a half dozen fish! How do you do it?"

The boy responds, "Roo raf roo reep ra rums rrarm."

"What was that?" asks the old man.

Again the boy responds, "Roo raf roo reep ra rums rrarm."

"Look," says the old man, "I can't understand a word you're saying."

The boy spits out the bait into his hand and says, "You have to keep the worms warm!"

As in many Canadian homes on New Year's Day, a man and his wife face the annual conflict over what is more important: the Canadian Junior games on television or New Year's Eve dinner. To keep peace, the husband has dinner with the rest of the family and even lingers for some pleasant after-dinner conversation before retiring to the family room in the basement to turn on the game.

A short time later, his wife goes downstairs and graciously brings her husband a cold drink. She smiles, kisses him on the cheek and asks what the score is. He tells her it is the end of the second period and that the score is still nothing to nothing.

"See?" she says. "You didn't miss a thing."

Bill: "Hey, Phil, are you going fishing?"
Phil: "Yah!"
Bill: "Ya got worms?"
Phil: "Yah, but I'm still going!"

## No Gators

While sports fishing off the Florida coast, a tourist capsizes his boat. The guy can swim, but his fear of alligators keeps him clinging to the overturned craft.

Spotting an old beachcomber standing on the shore, the tourist shouts, "Are there any gators around here?!"

"Nah," the man hollers back, "they ain't been around for years!"

Feeling safe, the tourist starts swimming leisurely toward the shore. About halfway there, he asks the guy, "How did you get rid of the gators?"

Q: What is the difference between Yankee fans and dentists?

A: One roots for the Yanks, and the other yanks for the roots.

"We didn't do nothin'," the beachcomber replies. "The sharks got 'em."

Jenny is taking her first skydiving lesson. The instructor tells her to jump out of the plane and pull her ripcord. After she's done that, the instructor jumps out of the plane after her. The instructor pulls the ripcord, but his parachute doesn't open. As he struggles to pull the emergency cord, he shoots down past Jenny. She undoes her straps on her own parachute and yells, "So, you wanna race?"

For sale: Parachute. Only used once, never opened, small stain.

Words to live by: Never argue with the person who packs your parachute.

Harry goes skydiving but nothing happens when he pulls his ripcord. He pulls the reserve, but it, too, is broken. Suddenly, Harry sees a man in blue overalls shooting up toward him.

"Hey!" shouts Harry. "Know anything about parachutes?"

"No!" yells the man. "Know anything about gas stoves?"

The dentist complimented the goalie on his nice, even teeth—one, three, seven, nine and eleven were missing.

No one has ever complained about a parachute not opening.

A man arrives at a soccer match midway through the second half.

"What's the score?" he asks.

"Nil, nil," comes the reply.

"Oh," says the man. "And what was the score at halftime?"

A boxer goes to a doctor complaining of insomnia.

"Have you tried counting sheep?" asks the doctor.

"It doesn't work," replies the boxer. "Every time I get to nine, I stand up."

Skydivers: Good to the last drop.

Billy: "My dad is really annoyed."

Joe: "Why? What happened?"

Billy: "I had the TV on the other night, and he accidentally saw the entire football game. He'd just wanted to watch the results on the news."

Q: Did you hear the one about the tap dancer who injured himself?

A: He slipped and fell in the sink.

Q: Why was the centipede dropped from the insect soccer team?

A: He took too long to put his boots on!

Headline News: There was a tragic end to the water polo championships—all the horses drowned.

*The hockey lockout has been settled. They have stopped bickering...and can now get down to some serious bloodshed.*

—Conan O'Brien, host of
*Late Night with Conan O'Brien*

Did you hear about the cowardly matador who used to go into the ring with a white sheet instead of a red cape? If things got rough, he surrendered.

A Canadian hockey fan and a British hockey fan are camped outside an ice arena waiting for the hockey players to come out. The Brit pulls out his packed lunch.

The Canadian asks, "What have you got?"

"Tongue sandwiches," replies the Brit.

"Yuck, I couldn't eat something that has come out of an animal's mouth!" says the Canadian.

"Well, what kind of sandwiches have you got then?" asks the Brit.

"Egg."

The increasingly murky water in the swimming pool worries the manager of a health spa, so he sends a sample off to the lab for analysis. A week later, he receives the report that says, "This horse is seriously ill and should be put down immediately."

Albert Einstein dies and goes to heaven, only to be informed that his room is not ready.

The doorman tells him, "I hope you don't mind waiting in a dormitory. We are very sorry, but it's the best we can do, and you will have to share the room with others."

> Boxing raises the consciousness.

Einstein says that this is no problem at all, and that there is no need to make such a great fuss. So, the doorman leads him to the dorm. They enter, and Albert is introduced to all the present inhabitants.

"Here is your first roommate. He has an IQ of 180!"

"Why, that's wonderful!" says Albert. "We can discuss mathematics!"

"And here is your second roommate. His IQ is 150!"

"Why, that's wonderful!" says Albert. "We can discuss physics!"

"And here is your third roommate. His IQ is 100!"

"That's wonderful! We can discuss the latest plays at the theatre!"

Just then, another man walks over to Albert and says, "I'm your fourth roommate, and I'm sorry, but my IQ is only 80."

Albert smiles at him and says, "So, where do you think the Blue Jays are headed this season?"

Jenny: "Where did you learn to swim?"

Gloria: "In the water."

The Pittsburgh Penguins and the Calgary Flames are in Pittsburgh playing a close game that is tied 1–1 late in the third period.

Just before a face-off, Jarome Iginla lines up next to Sidney Crosby and says, "Hey, Crosby, you're a Canadian and playing hockey in America, right?"

Crosby swells out his chest and says, "Damn right I am, and I'm proud of it."

Iginla smiles and quips, "Then what are you in the bathroom?"

Crosby looks at Iginla and, appearing confused, asks, "What?"

Iginla laughs and says, "European."

A football coach walks into the locker room before a game, looks over to his star player and says, "I'm not supposed to let you play since you failed math, but we need you in there. So I have to ask you a math question, and if you get it right, you can play."

The player agrees, so the coach looks into the player's eyes intently and asks, "Okay, now concentrate hard, and tell me the answer to this. What is two plus two?"

The player thinks for a moment and then answers, "Four?"

"Did you say four?" the coach exclaimed, excited that the player got it right.

Old soccer players never die; they just kick off.

Suddenly, all the other players on the team begin screaming, "Come on, Coach, give him another chance!"

Three guys enter a disabled swimming contest.

The first has no arms.

The second, no legs.

And the third has no body, just a head.

They all line up, the whistle blows and splash, they're all in the pool.

The guy with no arms takes the lead instantly, but the guy with no legs is closing fast. The head, of course, sinks straight to the bottom.

Ten lengths later, the guy with no legs finishes first. He can still see bubbles coming from the bottom of the pool, so he decides he'd better dive down to rescue the head.

Old golfers don't die! They just lose their drive.

He picks up the head, swims back up to the surface and places him at the side of the pool, whereupon he starts coughing and spluttering.

Eventually, the head catches his breath and shouts, "Three years I've spent learning to swim with my ears, then two seconds before the whistle, some idiot puts a swimming cap on me!"

"I thought I told you to keep an eye on your cousin," a mother says to her son. "Where is he?"

"Well," her son replies thoughtfully, "if he knows as much about canoeing as he thinks he does, he's out canoeing. If he knows as little as I think he does, he's out swimming."

If you jog backwards, will you gain weight?

## Top 10 Ways the Chicago Blackhawks Spend Their Time Off After Winning the Stanley Cup

10. Joyriding on the Zamboni.

9. Skeet shooting on the White House lawn.

8. Watching *Oprah*.

7. "You know that adorable skating bunny in the Ice Capades? That was me!"

6. Watching the tape of the 2010 playoffs 7000 times.

5. Crank-calling Sidney Crosby.

4. Playing golf with the Toronto Maple Leafs.

3. Eating!

2. Being a couch potato.

1. Partying with Don Cherry.

## Pink Basketballs

Every year, Jim's father asks him what he wants for his birthday, and every year Jim asks for a pink basketball. For years and years, this is the only gift Jim ever requests. While other kids want the latest toys or new electronics, Jim only wants a pink basketball. For his birthday, he wanted a pink basketball; for Christmas, he wanted a pink basketball.

His father tries to tempt him with the latest "in" thing, but nothing else tempts Jim.

> When the cannibals ate a missionary, they got a taste of religion.

Eventually, Jim's dad gets tired of buying his son pink basketballs, so for Jim's 18th birthday, his father surprises him with a brand new sports car. Jim likes the car and takes it into town for a spin. Passing a sports store, Jim sees that the store has some pink basketballs in the window, so he parks the car and crosses the street to take a better look. Halfway across the road, Jim is hit by a truck. Jim's father goes to see him in the hospital. He knows Jim isn't going to make it and wants to ask his son one question before he dies.

"Jim," he says. "You've never played basketball in your life, so why all these years did you want pink basketballs?"

Jim looks up at his father, opens his mouth to speak and dies. And the moral of the story is: Always look both ways before crossing the street.

## Putting Up with Jocks

A baseball coach storms into the principal's office and demands a raise right then and there.

"Please," protests the principal, "you already make more than the entire math department."

"Yah, maybe so, but you don't know what I have to put up with," the coach blusters. "Look." He goes out into the hall and grabs a jock, who is jogging down the hallway. "Run over to my office and see if I'm there," he orders.

Twenty minutes later, the jock returns, sweaty and out of breath. "You're not there, sir," he reports.

"Okay, I see what you mean," concedes the principal, scraching his head. "I would have phoned."

## The World of Bowling

- Bowling is a sport that should be right down your alley.

- If you can't hear a pin drop, something is definitely wrong with your bowling.

- Our small town used to have a bowling alley, but somebody stole the pin.

- I'll never bowl with him again. After he got a strike, he spiked the ball.

- If our town didn't have bowling, there'd be no culture at all.

- I go bowling once every four years to make sure I still hate it.

If a jogger were to run at the speed of sound, would he still hear his iPod?

Tom says to his friend, "My sister has taken up bodybuilding."

"Oh yeah? Does she like it?" asks the friend.

"Yeah, she's really good at it. In fact, she's so good, she's now my brother."

## Apology to Americans

*I'm sorry we beat you in Olympic hockey. In our defence, I guess our excuse would be that our team was much, much, much, much better than yours. By way of apology, please accept all of our Canadian NHL teams, which one by one are going out of business and moving to your fine country.*

–*This Hour Has Twenty Two Minutes*

## Trust Issues

There is a huge fire at the All-Star hockey game. Three hockey fans wearing the jerseys of their favourite teams are stranded on the roof: a Montreal Canadiens fan, a Boston Bruins fan and a Detroit Red Wings fan. The fire department arrives with a blanket and yells to the Canadiens fan to jump. He jumps, the firefighters move the blanket to the right and the fan hits the sidewalk with the splat. Then they call to the Boston fan to jump. He says that he won't jump. The firefighters explain

Be kind to animals.
Hug a hockey player.

that they hated the Canadiens. The fan says he hates them too and jumps. Again, the firefighters move the blanket to the right, and the fan hits the ground with a splat.

Finally, they call to the Detroit Red Wings fan to jump. He says he won't jump. The fire fighters say they really hate the Bruins.

The Detroit fan replies, "I don't trust you! Lay the blanket down, and then I'll jump!"

Three Canadians and three Americans are travelling to a hockey game by train. The three Americans each buy tickets then watch as the three Canadians buy only one.

"How are you going to travel on only one ticket?" asks an American.

"Watch and you'll see," says a Canadian.

They all board the train. The Americans take their respective seats, but all three Canadians cram into a bathroom and close the door.

Time flies like an arrow. Fruit flies like a banana.

Shortly after the train has departed, the conductor comes around collecting tickets. He knocks on the bathroom door and says, "Ticket, please!"

The door opens a crack, and a single arm emerges with a ticket in hand. The conductor takes it and moves on. The Americans see this and agree it is quite a clever idea. After the game, they decide to copy the Canadians on the return trip to save some money. When they get to the station, they buy a single ticket for the return trip. To their astonishment, the Canadians don't buy a ticket at all.

"How are you going to travel without a ticket?" asks one perplexed American.

"Watch and you'll see," replies a Canadian.

When they board the train, the three Americans cram themselves into a bathroom, and the three Canadians cram themselves into another bathroom nearby.

Once the train leaves the station, one of the Canadians leaves and walks over to the other bathroom where the Americans are hiding, knocks on the door and says, "Ticket, please!"

## CHAPTER SIX

# Fooood

Mrs. Miggins has a restaurant famous throughout the land. Travellers come from far and wide to eat her marvellous bean casserole. Many customers note that it doesn't make you fart like other bean stews.

Curious travellers ask, "Mrs. Miggins, why doesn't your bean casserole make people fart?"

Q: Why couldn't the orange cross the road?

A: Because it ran out of juice.

"Because I use exactly 239 beans."

"Just 239 beans? That seems very exact. Why 239?"

"Because one more would make it Two Forty."

First man: "Waiter, I'd like a cup of tea; make it weak and with lemon."

Second man: "I'd like tea, too, but strong, with no lemon, and, waiter, please make sure the cup is sparkling clean."

Q: Why can't you tell a secret in a cornfield?

A: Too many ears are listening.

(Ten minutes later)

Waiter: "Here we are, gentlemen. Now, which one of you gets the clean cup?"

Q: Why don't lobsters share?

A: Because they're shellfish.

A man walks into a restaurant in downtown Halifax and orders a cup of coffee. When it arrives, he pours the coffee into an ashtray and eats the cup and saucer, leaving only the cup handle behind. He then calls the waiter over and orders another coffee. As soon as the coffee is put down, the man pours the coffee out and eats the cup and saucer. An hour later, he has a pile of cup handles in front of him.

The man turns to the waiter and says, "You think I'm crazy, don't you?"

The waiter replies, "Yes, sir, the handles are the best part!"

A woman has to lose 20 pounds, so her doctor tells her to eat nothing but rice cakes for a month. After a month, she goes back to the doctor, who is amazed to find that she has gained 15 pounds.

Q: How does a moulded fruit-flavoured dessert answer the phone?

A: Jell-o!

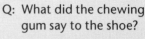

"What happened?" asks the doctor. "Were you were not eating the rice cakes? Did you find them too boring?"

Q: What did the chewing gum say to the shoe?

A: I'm stuck on you.

"At first they were," says the woman, "but they tasted much better after I started dipping them in chocolate."

College student: "Mom, can you make me old, cold, reheated coffee in a chipped cup, last week's meatloaf with a bottle of ketchup on the side and a couple of slices of bread with the mouldy parts cut off?"

Mom: "Oh, why would you eat that?"

College student: "That's a good meal in college."

Did you hear about the new cannibal restaurant that costs an arm and a leg?

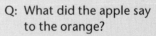

Q: What did the apple say to the orange?

A: Nothing, silly, apples don't talk.

A man orders a steak at a restaurant but notices that the waiter bringing it to his table is pressing the steak to the plate with his thumb.

"That's very unhygienic," complains the man.

"It'll be more unhygienic if I drop it again," replies the waiter.

A restaurant customer asks to see the manager and says, "This place is filthy."

"That's an outrageous statement," replies the manager. "You could eat your dinner off our floor."

"That's the problem," replies the customer. "It looks like someone has."

Q: What did baby corn say to Mama corn?
A: Where is popcorn?

Q: What do you call a fake noodle?
A: An impasta.

A kid goes to a seafood restaurant in Saint John with his parents and orders a fresh salmon.

The waiter comes over and says, "I'm sorry for the delay with your order, young man, it should be here shortly."

The kid replies, "That's okay, but if you don't mind my asking, what sort of bait are you using?

Bert: "Hey, Ernie, do you want some ice cream?"
Ernie: "Sure, Bert!"

A man grabs a bowl and a spoon and goes outside. Then one of his

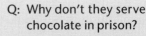

Q: Why don't they serve chocolate in prison?

A: Because it makes you break out.

friends comes over to see him, and asks the man why he has a bowl and a spoon outside.

The man replies, "I listened to the weather channel, and they said it was going to be…chili!"

A woman rushes to her dietician. "You've got to help me. This diet you put me on is making me irritable. Yesterday, I bit someone's ear off."

"Oh no," replies the dietician. "That's a lot of calories."

A boy gets a new Thermos from his mom. "Here you go, Billy. This will keep hot things hot and cold things cold," she says.

Little Billy takes it to school the next day. "Look at this," he says to his friend over lunch.

Q: What happens to a hamburger that misses a lot of school?

A: He has a lot of ketchup time.

"It's a Thermos, and it keeps hot things hot and cold things cold."

"What have you got inside?" asks his friend.

"Two hot chocolates and a scoop of vanilla ice cream."

"We've got a new toaster," says a little boy to his friend. "It's really smart. When the toast is done, a bell rings."

"Ours is better," says his friend. "When the toast is done, it sends out smoke signals."

Q: What did the hamburger name his daughter?

A: Patty.

A woman is looking through the frozen turkeys at the supermarket but can't find one big enough for her family.

She calls over to the grocer and asks, "Do these turkeys get any bigger?"

"No," the grocer replies, "they're dead."

Q: What kind of egg did the bad chicken lay?

A: A devilled egg.

A man goes into a restaurant and asks, "How do you prepare the chicken?"

"We don't," replies the waiter. "We just tell it straight up that it's going to die."

Q: What kind of cake do you get at a cafeteria?

A: A stomach-cake.

A man walks into a seafood restaurant and sees a sign saying: "Lobster Tails, $1 each."

The man asks the waitress, "Those must be very small tails if you're selling them so cheaply."

"No, they are all normal size," replies the waitress.

"Then they have to be pretty old," says the man.

"No, they are fresh today."

"There must be something wrong with them," says the man.

"No, they are just regular lobster tails," says the waitress.

"Okay," says the man. "I'll have one."

Q: Why did the cookie go to the hospital?

A: It felt crummy.

Q: Are hamburgers male or female?

A: Male, because they're called boygers, not girlgers!

So the waitress takes the man's money, sits down beside the man and says, "Once upon a time, there was a big red lobster…"

Mother says to a friend: "My son attended the karate school of cooking. He could kill with just one chop."

A hole has been found in the nudist camp wall. The police are looking into it.

Two potato chips are walking down the street. One is assaulted.

*I bought some powdered water. But I don't know what to add.*

—Steven Wright, comedian

Two fish swim into a concrete wall. One turns to the other and says, "Dam!"

Eating vegetables is much crueller than eating animals. At least the animals have a chance to run away.

To attract a vegetarian, make a noise like a wounded vegetable.

There is a farmer in BC who grows apples. He is doing pretty well, but he is annoyed because some local kids are sneaking into his orchard at night and eating his apples.

After some careful thought, he has a clever idea to scare the kids away for sure. He constructs a sign and posts it in his orchard. The next day, the kids show up and they see his sign: "Warning: One of the apple trees in this field has been injected with poison."

> Q: How do you make a hot-dog stand?
>
> A: Steal its chair.

> Q: What do snowmen eat for breakfast?
>
> A: Snowflakes.

The kids are pretty bright and not about to risk taking another apple. They run off, make their own sign and post it next to the farmer's sign.

The next day, the farmer shows up to look over his orchard, and he notices to his delight that no apples are missing. He is perplexed, however, by the new sign next to his. He drives his tractor up to the sign that reads: "Now, there are two!"

*I like baked potatoes, man. I don't have a micro-wave oven. It takes forever to cook a baked potato in*

*a conventional oven. Sometimes I'll just throw one in there, even if I don't want one. By the time it's done, who knows.*

–Mitch Hedberg, comedian

A young man goes into a Dairy Queen and asks, "What kinds of ice cream do you have?"

"Vanilla, chocolate, strawberry," the girl wheezes as she pats her chest and seems unable to continue.

A vulture carrying two dead raccoons boards an airplane. The flight attendant looks at him and says, "I'm sorry, sir, only one carrion allowed per passenger."

"Do you have laryngitis?" the young man asks sympathetically.

"Nope," she whispers, "just vanilla, chocolate and strawberry."

Q: Why did the baby blueberry cry?
A: Because his mother was in a jam.

Waiter: "May I tell you about our corn on the cob?"

Customer: "Yes. Give me an earful."

Customer: "I'd like some coffee!"
Waiter: "How do you want it?"
Customer: "In a cup."

After a delicious lunch in an Italian restaurant, a well-travelled businesswoman calls the chef over to compliment him on the meal.

"Your eggplant parmesan was better than the one I ate in Milan last Tuesday," she tells him.

Q: What do you say to a hamburger?

A: How, now, ground cow.

"It's not surprising," says the chef proudly. "They use domestic cheese. Here we use imported!"

If we aren't supposed to eat animals, why are they made of meat?

## A Day at the Ball Park

A doctor at an insane asylum decides to take his patients to see a Blue Jays game. For weeks in advance, he coaches his patients to respond to his commands. When the day of the game arrives, everything seems to be going well.

Q: A little girl is sitting in the kitchen, eating a popsicle. Her mom walks in behind her and scares her, so she drops it. What does the little girl have?

A: A DROP-sicle!

As the Canadian national anthem starts, the doctor yells, "Up, nuts!"

All the patients obey and stand up.

After the anthem, the doctor yells, "Down, nuts!"

They all sit back down in their seats.

After a home run, the doctor yells, "Cheer, nuts!"

They all break out into applause and cheer.

When the umpire makes a particularly bad call against the star of the home team, the doctor yells, "Boooo, nuts!"

The patients all start booing.

Thinking things are going very well, the doctor decides to go get a Coke and a hot dog, leaving his assistant in charge. When the doctor returns, there is a riot in progress.

Finding his assistant, the doctor asks, "What in the world happened?"

The assistant replies, "Well, everything was going just fine until a vendor passed by and yelled, 'PEANUTS!'"

Q: What do you call artificial spaghetti?

A: Mockaroni.

Q: What does the sun drink out of?

A: Sunglasses.

Q: What do rap singers eat for breakfast?

A: Cheeri-yo's!

## CHAPTER SEVEN

# Boys and Girls

## The White Knight

Once upon a time, there was a famous white knight who desired to wed a beautiful princess. So one day, he rides to the castle where the princess lives to seek permission from her father, the wise king.

"Who goes there?" demands the gatekeeper.

"It is the white knight on the white horse," replies the knight. "I wish to see the king."

"Not *the* white knight on *the* white horse?" says the gatekeeper.

"Yes, *the* white knight on *the* white horse."

"Very well. You may enter the castle."

The knight walks through the castle to the chamber of the king.

"Who disturbs the king?" bellows his royal highness.

"It is I, the white knight on the white horse. I have come to ask for the hand of your daughter, the Princess Guinevere."

"Not *the* white knight on *the* white horse?" says the king.

"Yes, *the* white knight on *the* white horse."

"Well, before you can marry my daughter, you must obtain the golden ring from the lair of the evil golden dragon."

"I shall do that," replies the knight, and he rides toward the distant lands where lives the evil dragon.

The golden dragon is in his lair.

"Who lurks outside my home?" it calls out into the darkness at the sound of the approaching knight.

"It is I, the white knight on the white horse. I have come to claim the golden ring with which I may marry the king's daughter, the Princess Guinevere."

"Not *the* white knight on *the* white horse?" asks the golden dragon.

"Yes, *the* white knight on *the* white horse," replies the knight with a sigh.

Without putting up a fight, the golden dragon hands him the ring, and the knight rides back to the castle.

"Who goes there?" demands the gatekeeper.

"It is the white knight on the white horse."

"Did you say *the* white knight on *the* white horse?"

"Yes, *the* white knight on *the* white horse. I am here to see the king."

"Come on through, white knight on the white horse."

The white knight enters the castle and knocks on the king's chamber door.

"Who is there?" bellows the king.

"It is the white knight on the white horse."

"Did you just say *the* white knight on *the* white horse?"

"Oh god," the knight whispers to himself. "Yes, sire, it is *the* white knight on *the* white horse."

The king opens the door, and the knight enters.

"I have obtained the golden ring from the dragon. Now may I ask for the princess' hand in marriage?"

"Before you can marry my daughter," replies the king, "you must retrieve the ruby ring from the evil troll."

"I shall do that," says the knight, and he rides off in search of the evil troll.

The knight travels deep into the forest and comes upon the lair of the evil troll.

"Who disturbs my peace?" says the troll.

"It is the white knight on the white horse. I have come to take the ruby ring from you so that I may marry the king's daughter."

A chicken crossing the road is poultry in motion.

"Not *the* white knight on *the* white horse?"

"Yes, *the* white knight on *the* white horse."

Fearing for his life, the troll hands over the ruby ring to the white knight of legend. The knight rides off toward the castle.

"Who goes there?" demands the gatekeeper.

"It is the white knight on the white horse."

"Did you say *the* white knight on *the* white horse?"

"Yes, *the* white knight on *the* white horse. I am here to see the king."

"Come on through, white knight on the white horse."

The white knight enters the castle and knocks on the king's chamber door.

"Who is it?" says the king.

"It is the white knight on the white horse. I have come to deliver the ruby ring and ask for your daughter's hand in marriage."

The king opens the chamber door.

"Very well, brave white knight on the white horse," says the king. "You have obtained the rings as I asked of you. Go now to the north tower and ask for Princess Guinevere's hand in marriage."

The knight is escorted to the princess' chamber and knocks on her door.

"Who is it?" says Princess Guinevere.

"It is the white knight on the white horse."

"Not *the* white knight on *the* white horse?"

"Yes, *the* white knight on *the* white horse."

The princess opens the chamber door. Never before has the knight seen such a beautiful woman in his life.

"Your father, the king, has given me permission to ask for your hand in marriage. So, Princess Guinevere, will you marry me?" asks the knight.

"No."

A young man makes a promise to his girlfriend. "We're going to have such a great time Saturday. I got three tickets for the big hockey game."

"Why do you have three tickets?" she asks.

"One for your mother, one for your father and one for your little brother."

A guy is driving in a car with his blonde girlfriend. He tells her to stick her head out the window and see if the blinker works.

She sticks her head out and says, "Yes... no...yes...no...yes..."

Bernie invites his friend Morris home for dinner. During dinner, Morris precedes every

Q: Did you hear about the girl who started dating a boy and then found out he had a wooden leg?

A: She broke it off, of course.

request to his girlfriend with endearing terms, calling her Honey, My Love, Darling, Sweetheart, Pumpkin and so on.

Bernie looks at Morris and says, "It's really nice that after all these years you have been together, you keep calling your girlfriend those pet names."

Morris hangs his head and whispers, "To tell the truth, I forgot her name three years ago…"

Cannibal #1: "I really hate my sister."
Cannibal #2: "Well, just eat the vegetables then."

Q: Why did the little boy put his sister's lipstick on his head?

A: He wanted to make up his mind.

Daniel has a girlfriend named Lorraine. She is very pretty, and he likes her a lot. One day he goes to work to find that a new girl has started work at his office. Her name is Clearly, and she is absolutely gorgeous. He begins to like her, and after a while, it becomes obvious that she is interested in him, too. But Daniel is a loyal man and won't get involved with Clearly while he is still going out with Lorraine. He decides that there is nothing for him to do but to break up with Lorraine and date the new girl. He plans several times to tell Lorraine, but he can't bring himself to do it. One day, as they are walking along the river bank, Lorraine falls into the river. The current carries her and she drowns. Daniel stops for a moment by the river and then runs off, smiling and singing, "I can see Clearly now Lorraine is gone…"

A teenager goes to an Internet dating site to find the perfect girlfriend. He types in that he wants someone who is small and cute. She must love water sports and enjoy group activities. He then hits "Enter" and waits for the computer to find his perfect match. Ten seconds later, a picture of a penguin comes on screen.

A lonely frog goes to a fortune teller.

"You're going to meet a beautiful young girl who will want to know everything about you," says the fortune teller.

The frog is thrilled. "This is fantastic! Will I meet her at a party?"

"No," replies the fortune teller, "in biology class."

A mushroom walks into a restaurant. He sits next to a beautiful woman and tries to pick her up. He gives her a few corny lines, but she says, "Get out of here, I don't want anything to do with you!"

The mushroom replies, "What's the matter? I'm a fun-gi!"

One Sunday morning, a little girl dressed in her Sunday best is running so she won't be late for church.

As she runs, she keeps saying, "Dear God, please don't let me be late to church. Please don't let me be late to church..."

As she is running, she trips and falls.

When she gets back up, she begins praying again, "Please, God, don't let me be late to church, but don't shove me either!"

A reason Santa has to be a man: No woman is going to wear the same outfit, year after year.

A Sunday school teacher is discussing the Ten Commandments with her five- and six-year-olds.

After explaining the commandment to "honour thy father and thy mother," she asks, "Is there a commandment that teaches us how to treat our brothers and sisters?"

Without missing a beat, one little boy answers, "Thou shall not kill."

Any father will tell you that parents spend the first two or three years of their daughters' lives trying to teach them to talk and the next 15 or so trying to get them to shut up.

Four-year-old Mitch loves candy almost as much as his mom, Ann, does. So for Valentine's Day, he and his daddy give Ann a beautiful heart-shaped box of chocolates. A few days later, Mitch is eyeing it, wishing to have a piece of it.

As he reaches out to touch one of the big pieces, Ann says to him, "If you touch it, then you have to eat it. Do you understand?"

"Oh, yes," he says, nodding his head. Suddenly, his little hand pats the tops of all the pieces of candy. "Now I can eat them all."

## CHAPTER EIGHT

# Parents Just Don't Get It

A little girl has made a fresh cup of tea for her mother.

"I didn't know you could make tea," says the little girl's mother, taking a sip.

"Yes, I boiled some water, added the tea leaves like you do and then strained it into a cup. But I couldn't find the strainer, so I used the fly swatter."

"Acckk!" screams the mother, spitting out the tea.

"Oh, don't worry, Mother. I didn't use the new fly swatter. I used the old one."

A little boy runs home and confesses to his mother that he broke a vase at his friend's house.

"Don't be upset, Mom," says the boy. "You don't have to buy a new one because Timmy's mom said it was 'irreplaceable.'"

A fellow looking for a room for himself and his family calls a motel in Newfoundland and asks how much they charge for a room. The clerk tells him that the rates depend on the room size and the number of people staying in the room.

"Do you take children?" the man asks.

"No, sir," replies the clerk. "Only cash or credit cards."

Bored out of his mind, a small boy is acting up in church during the Sunday morning service. His constant talking and laughing begins to upset the other worshippers. His father finally loses his patience and starts to drag the young boy out of the church. On the way down the aisle, the boy shouts out to the congregation, "Pray for me!"

Noticing that his four-year-old daughter is tired from playing all day at the park, her father picks her up and puts her on his shoulders. After a few minutes, she starts pulling and tugging his hair.

"Ouch! Stop that, sweetheart," he says. "It hurts Daddy."

"But Daddy," she says, "I'm only trying to get my gum back."

## He Speaks!

Once there was a boy who never spoke. For the first few years of his life, his parents just figured he was a late bloomer. When he was still silent at the age of five, his parents began to worry and took him to all kinds of doctors, speech therapists and psychiatrists, but none could figure out why the boy remained silent.

Time passed, and the parents accepted that their son would never speak. Then one day, on his eighth birthday, the boy's mother pours him a glass of milk to wash down his birthday cake, and immediately after taking one sip, the boy says, "This milk is sour."

Astonished, the parents can hardly believe their ears, "But you can talk! Why have you waited so long to talk to us?"

"Up until now," he says, "everything's been okay."

## For Your Parents

Whenever your children are out of control, you can take comfort from the thought that even God's omnipotence did not extend to his own children.

After creating heaven and earth, God created Adam and Eve, and the first thing he said was, "Don't."

"Don't what?" Adam replied.

"Don't eat the forbidden fruit," said God.

"Forbidden fruit? We have forbidden fruit? Hey, Eve...we have forbidden fruit!"

"No way!"

"Yes way!"

"Do NOT eat the fruit!" said God.

"Why?"

"Because I am your Father, and I said so!" God replied, wondering why he didn't stop creation after making the elephants.

A few minutes later, God saw his children having an apple break, and he was ticked! "Didn't I tell you not to eat the fruit?" God asked.

"Uh-huh," Adam replied.

"Then why did you?" asked the Father.

"I don't know," replied Eve.

"She started it!" said Adam.

"Did not!"

"Did too!"

"DID NOT!"

Having had it with the two of them, God's punishment was that Adam and Eve should have children of their own.

Thus, the pattern was set, and it has never changed! But there is reassurance in this story. If you have persistently and lovingly tried to give children wisdom and they haven't taken it, don't be hard on yourself. If God had trouble raising children, what made you think it would be a piece of cake for you?

Mother has just finished waxing the floors when she hears her young son opening the front door.

She shouts, "Be careful on that floor, Jimmy! It's just been waxed."

Jimmy, walking right in, replies, "Don't worry, Mom, I'm wearing my cleats!"

Ozzie comes home from school with a black eye and a cut lip.

His mother sighs deeply and says, "Oh, Ozzie, you've been in another fight."

"But, Mom," sniffles Ozzie, "I was just keeping a little boy from being beaten up by a bigger boy."

'Well," says the mom, "that was brave. Who was the little boy?"

"Me, Mommy."

Two Eskimos sitting in a kayak were chilly, so they lit a fire in the craft. Not surprisingly, it sank, proving once again that you can't have your kayak and heat it too.

## Come Out, Come Out

A boss urgently needs to speak to one of his employees on the weekend and calls him at home.

The employee's son answers the phone with a whisper.

"Hello," says the boss. "Is your daddy home?"

"Yes," whispers the boy.

"Then may I speak to him?"

"No."

"Well, then can I talk to your mommy?"

"No."

Thinking it strange that the boy is left home alone, the boss asks again, "Well, is anyone home?"

"Yes, a policeman," says the boy in a whisper.

The boss is startled. "Can I speak with the police officer?"

"No, he's busy," whispers the boy.

"Busy doing what?" asks the boss with concern in his voice.

"The policeman is busy talking to Daddy, Mommy and another policeman," says the boy.

> Q: How do you get your dad to do sit-ups?
> A: Put the remote control between his toes.

The boss then hears the sound of a helicopter in the background. "Is that a helicopter?"

"Yes," replies the boy.

"Young man, what exactly is going on at home?" asks the boss.

"The search team just landed," says the boy.

"What! A search team! What are they looking for?"

"Shhh! It's hide and seek, and they're looking for me."

## Twins

A woman has twins and gives them up for adoption. One of them goes to a family in Egypt and is named Amal. The other goes to a family in Spain; they name him Juan. Years later, Juan sends a picture of himself to his birth mother. Upon receiving the picture, she tells her husband that she wishes she also had a picture of Amal.

Her husband responds, "But they're twins. If you've seen Juan, you've seen Amal."

Son: "Mom, the new baby looks just like the dog."

Mom: "Son, don't say such things!"

Son: "It's okay, Mom. The dog can't hear me."

A family puts their house up for sale, and the mother stresses emphatically to her 15-year-old son that he make his bed each morning so that the house looks presentable when the real estate agent shows it to prospective buyers.

Day after day, she is surprised and impressed to find her son's bed is perfectly made. That night, she goes into his room and discovers his secret.

She finds her son fast asleep on the floor in his sleeping bag.

Two mothers are sitting in a park in Toronto watching their kids play.

First mother: "What are your kids' names?"

Second mother: "Richard, Jimmy, Sally, Marie and Wing Mei."

First mother: "Wing Mei is an unusual name compared to Richard and Sally."

Second mother: "Well, my husband and I read that every fifth baby born in the world is Chinese."

One day, a father comes home with a big bag of candy and says to his kids, "I'm going to give these to the person who never talks back to Mommy and always does what they are told. Now, who's going to get them?"

The kids answer, "You are!"

A young couple bring their new baby home, and the wife suggests that her husband try his hand at changing a diaper.

"I'm busy," he says. "I'll do the next one."

The next time the baby's diaper needs changing, the wife asks her husband to do it.

The husband says, "I didn't mean the next diaper. I meant the next baby."

A father and son are out fishing.

The boy asks, "Dad, how do boats float?"

"I don't know," replies the dad.

"How do fish breathe?" asks the son.

"I don't know," replies the dad.

"Why is the sky blue?" says the son.

"I don't know," replies the dad.

"Dad," says the boy, "I hope you don't mind me asking you all these questions."

"Of course not," replies the dad. "If you don't ask questions, how will you ever learn anything?"

## Famous Mothers

ALBERT EINSTEIN'S MOTHER: "But, Albert, it's your senior picture. Can't you do something about your hair? Styling gel, mousse, something...?"

SUPERMAN'S MOTHER: "Clark, your father and I have discussed it, and we've decided you can have your own telephone line. Now will you quit spending so much time in all those phone booths?"

BARNEY'S MOTHER: "I realize strained plums are your favourite, Barney, but you're starting to look a little purple."

MICHELANGELO'S MOTHER: "Mike, can't you paint on walls like other kids? Do you have any idea how hard it is to get that stuff off the ceiling?"

MONA LISA'S MOTHER: "After all that money your father and I spent on braces, Mona, that's the biggest smile you can give us?"

HUMPTY DUMPTY'S MOTHER: "Humpty, if I've told you once, I've told you a hundred times, do not sit on that wall. But will you listen to me? Noooo!"

COLUMBUS' MOTHER: "I don't care what you've discovered, Christopher. You still could have written!"

Julie: "Daddy, why is Mommy singing?"

Daddy: "So your baby sister will go to sleep."

Julie: "Will Mommy stop singing when the baby is asleep?"

Daddy: "Yes, dear."

Julie: "Then why doesn't the baby just pretend to be asleep?"

Jenny: "I can't get a babysitter who actually pays attention to the kids!"

Martha: "Oh, I solved that problem. I just put the baby on top of the TV!"

Mom: "I'm tired of cleaning up your room. I've decided to charge you 10 cents every time I have to pick something up off the floor. So far, you owe me two dollars."

Son: "Here it is, Mom. Keep up the good work."

## Goodbye, Mother!

Walking through a supermarket, a young man notices an elderly woman following him around. He ignores her for a while, but when he gets to the checkout line, she gets in front of him.

"Pardon me," she says. "I'm sorry if I've been staring, but you look just like my son who died recently."

"I'm sorry for your loss," the young man replies. "Is there anything I can do for you?"

"Well, as I'm leaving, could you just say 'Goodbye, Mother.' It would make me feel so much better," the woman says, as she gives him a sweet smile.

"Of course I can," the young man promises.

As the old lady gathers her bags and is walking out of the store, he calls out to her, "Goodbye, Mother!" just as she had requested, and he feels good about her smile.

Stepping up to the counter, the young man sees that the total for his groceries is about $100 higher than it should be.

"That amount is wrong," he says to the clerk. "I have only a few items!"

"Oh, your mother said that you would pay for hers," explains the clerk.

Two children order their mother to stay in bed one Mother's Day morning. As she lies there looking forward to breakfast, the smell of bacon floats up from the kitchen. After a good long wait, she finally goes downstairs to investigate. She finds her two children both sitting at the table eating bacon and eggs.

"As a surprise for Mother's Day," one explains, "we decided to cook our own breakfast."

While at the beach with his friend, Timmy says, "My mom said she learned how to swim when someone took her out on the lake in a boat and threw her overboard."

His friend replies, "They weren't trying to teach her how to swim."

After tucking their three-year-old child, Sammy, in bed one night, his parents hear sobbing coming from his room.

Rushing back into Sammy's room, they find him crying hysterically. Sammy tells them that he swallowed a penny, and he is sure he is going to die. No amount of talk helps.

His father, in an attempt to calm him down, takes a penny from his pocket without Sammy seeing and pretends to pull the penny from Sammy's ear. Sammy is delighted.

In a flash, Sammy snatches the penny from his father's hand, swallows it, and then cheerfully demands, "Do it again, Dad!"

# Things My Mother Taught Me...

1. My mother taught me TO APPRECIATE A JOB WELL DONE: "If you're going to kill each other, do it outside. I just finished cleaning."

2. My mother taught me RELIGION: "You'd better pray that stain will come out of the carpet."

3. My mother taught me about TIME TRAVEL: "If you don't straighten up, I'm going to knock you into the middle of next week."

4. My mother taught me REASON: "Because I said so, that's why."

5. My mother taught me LOGIC: "If you fall out of that swing and break your neck, you're not going to the store with me."

6. My mother taught me FORESIGHT: "Make sure you wear clean underwear, in case you're in an accident."

7. My mother taught me IRONY: "Keep crying, and I'll give you something to cry about."

8. My mother taught me about the science of OSMOSIS: "Shut your mouth and eat your supper."

9. My mother taught me about CONTORTIONISM: "Will you look at that dirt on the back of your neck?"

10. My mother taught me about STAMINA: "You'll sit there until all that spinach is gone."

11. My mother taught me about WEATHER: "This room of yours looks like a tornado went through it."

12. My mother taught me about HYPOCRISY: "If I've told you once, I've told you a million times. Don't exaggerate!"

13. My mother taught me about the CIRCLE OF LIFE: "I brought you into this world, and I can take you out."

14. My mother taught me about BEHAVIOUR MODIFICATION: "Stop acting like your father."

15. My mother taught me about ENVY: "There are millions of less fortunate children in this world who don't have wonderful parents like you do."

16. My mother taught me about ANTICIPATION: "Just wait until we get home."

17. My mother taught me about RECEIVING: "You are going to get it when you get home."

18. My mother taught me MEDICAL SCIENCE: "If you don't stop crossing your eyes, they are going to freeze that way."

19. My mother taught me ESP: "Put your sweater on; don't you think I know when you're cold?"

20. My mother taught me HUMOUR: "When that lawn mower cuts off your toes, don't come running to me."

21. My mother taught me HOW TO BECOME AN ADULT: "If you don't eat your vegetables, you'll never grow up."

A lumberjack had raised his only son and had managed to finance the young man's college education by the only way he knew how, cutting down trees, by hand.

The young man had helped his father cut down some of those trees. He knew how hard his father had to work to put him through school.

When the son started college, he promised himself the first thing he would do was buy his father a present that would make the old man's life easier. The son saved and scrimped and finally had enough money to purchase the finest chainsaw in the world.

On a school vacation, the son asks his dad how many trees he can cut down in one day. The father, a large husky man, thinks and says that on a good day, he can bring down 20 trees. The son gives the father the brand new chainsaw and says from now on he'll be able to triple the amount and work only half as hard.

The old man is very pleased and says he has the best son in the world. The young man leaves for school the next morning and isn't able to return until the next school break, three months later.

When he arrives home, he immediately notices that his dad appears rundown. He asks if his father is feeling all right. The old man replies that cutting trees is getting harder and harder, and now with the new chainsaw, he is working longer hours but not cutting as many trees as before.

The son knows there is something wrong and thinks perhaps the saw he purchased isn't as good as advertised. He asks to check it out. Upon examining the chainsaw, he checks the oiler and it is full. He checks the gas and it too is full. He yanks on the cord, and immediately, the saw roars to life.

His father grabs him by the shirt and hollers, "WHAT'S THAT NOISE?!"

Two young Alberta brothers are knocking around one lazy summer day and think it would be a good prank to push over the outhouse. They creep up from an advantageous direction like a couple of commandos, push the outhouse over on one side and head for the woods. They circle round and return home an hour later from a completely different direction, thus trying to divert suspicion from themselves.

Upon returning, their father approaches them with switch in hand and yells, "Did you two push the outhouse over this afternoon?"

The older boy replies, "As learned in school, I cannot tell a lie. Yes, Father, we pushed over the outhouse this afternoon."

At this revelation, the farmer sends them to bed without supper.

In the morning, the two boys meekly approach the breakfast table and take their seats. Everything is quiet until their father finally says, "Have you two learned your lesson?"

"Sure, Dad," says the big brother. "But in school we learned that George Washington admitted to his father that he'd chopped down a cherry tree, and he was forgiven because he told the truth."

"Ah, yes!' replies the farmer, "But George's dad wasn't in the cherry tree when he chopped it down!"

A mother is telling her little girl what her own childhood was like: "We used to skate outside on a pond. I had a swing made from a tire; it hung from a tree in our front yard. We rode our pony. We picked wild raspberries in the woods."

The little girl was wide-eyed, taking this in. At last she says, "I sure wish I'd gotten to know you sooner!"

Sunday school teacher: "Now, Johnny, tell me truthfully, do you say prayers before eating?"

Little Johnny: "No, sir. I don't have to. My mom is a good cook!"

# Top Ten Things You'll Never Hear Your Dad Say

10. "Well, how 'bout that? I'm lost! Looks like we'll have to stop and ask for directions."

9. "You know, Pumpkin, now that you're 13, you're ready for unchaperoned car dates. Won't that be fun?"

8. "I noticed that all your friends have a certain 'up yours' attitude. I like that."

7. "Here's a credit card and the keys to my new car. GO CRAZY!"

6. "What do you mean you wanna play football? Figure skating not good enough for you, son?"

5. "Your mother and I are going away for the weekend. You might want to consider throwing a party."

4. "Well, I don't know what's wrong with your car. Probably one of those doo-hickey thingies, you know, that makes it run or something. Just have it towed to a mechanic and pay whatever he asks."

3. "No son of mine is going to live under this roof without an earring. Now quit your bellyaching, and let's go to the mall."

2. "Whaddya wanna get a job for? I make plenty of money for you to spend."

1. "Father's Day? Aahh...don't worry about that. It's no big deal."

# Things Mothers Will Never Say

"Be good, and for your birthday I'll buy you a motorcycle!"

"How on earth can you see the TV sitting so far back?"

"Don't bother wearing a jacket; it's quite warm out."

"Let me smell that shirt. Yeah, it's good for another week."

"I think a cluttered bedroom is a sign of creativity."

"Yeah, I used to skip school, too."

"Just leave all the lights on. It makes the house more cheery."

"Could you turn the music up louder so I can enjoy it, too?"

"Run and bring me the scissors! Hurry!"

"Aw, just turn these undies inside out. No one will ever know."

"I don't have a tissue with me; just use your sleeve."

"Well, if Timmy's mom says it's okay, that's good enough for me."

"Of course you should walk to school and back. What's the big deal about having to cross a few main streets?"

"My meeting won't be over till later tonight. You kids don't mind if we skip dinner?"

## CHAPTER NINE

# Science and Technology

## Why It's a Mistake to Rely on Your Spell Checker

I halve a spelling checker. It came with my pea see. It plainly marks four my revue Mistakes I dew knot sea. Eye strike a key and type a word and weight four it two say weather eye am wrong oar write. It shows me strait aweigh. As soon as a mist ache is maid, it nose bee fore two long and eye can put the era rite. It's rarely ever wrong.

Black holes really suck.

I've scent this massage threw it, and I'm shore your pleased too no, its letter prefect in every weigh. My checker tolled me sew.

Scientists are preparing an experiment to ask the ultimate question. They have worked for months gathering one each of all the computers ever built. Finally, the big day is at hand. All the computers are linked together.

Q: Where do you go if you become "at one" with your computer?

A: Nerdvana.

The scientists ask the question, "IS THERE A GOD?"

Suddenly, there is a loud crash, and in a brilliant explosion of silicon and plastic, the computers fuse into what appears to the scientists to be one large computer in place of the many smaller ones. One of the scientists races to the printer as it finally outputs its answer.

"THERE IS NOW," reads the printout.

A blonde turns on the computer without the keyboard plugged in. When she turns on the computer, the computer gives a "Keyboard Error" message.

She then asks, "Why did it give me a keyboard error message? There isn't even one attached!"

Q: Why did the boy tiptoe past the medicine cabinet?

A: He didn't want to wake the sleeping pills.

Tom is trying to get his new computer working. He's having trouble, so he calls his friend Jay over to give him a hand. Jay switches on the computer, then asks Tom if he wants it password protected.

"Oh yes, I read about that in the manual. I think the password will be, "HomerBartLisaMarge-Maggie."

"That's a very long password," says Jay.

"Yes," replies Tom. "But the manual says it has to be at least four characters long."

Computer users are divided into three types: novice, intermediate and expert.

Novice users are people who are afraid that simply pressing a key might break their computer.

Intermediate users are people who don't know how to fix their computers after they've just pressed a key that broke it.

> Q: Why did the scientist install a knocker on his door?
>
> A: To win the nobell prize.

Expert users are people who break other people's computers.

## The Writer

There was once a man who, in his youth, professed his desire to become a great writer.

When asked to define "great," he said, "I want to write stuff that the whole world will read, stuff that people will react to on a truly emotional level, stuff that will make them scream, cry and howl in pain and anger!"

He now works for Microsoft, writing error messages.

## Bill Gates

Bill Gates dies in a car accident. He finds himself in purgatory, being sized up by St. Peter. "Well, Bill, I'm really confused on this call. I'm not sure whether to send you to heaven or hell. After all, you helped society a lot by putting a computer in almost every home in America, yet you also created that ghastly Windows 95. I'm going to do something I've never done before. I'm going to let you decide where you want to go."

Bill replies, "Well, what's the difference between the two?"

St. Peter says, "I'm willing to let you visit both places briefly, if it will help your decision."

A class on time travel will be held two weeks ago...

"Fine, but where should I go first?"

"I'll leave that up to you."

"Okay then," replies Bill, "Let's try hell first." So Bill goes to hell. It has a beautiful, clean, sandy beach with clear waters and lots of beautiful women running around, laughing and playing in the water. The sun is shining, and the temperature is perfect. Bill is very pleased.

"This is great!" he tells St. Peter. "If this is hell, I REALLY want to see heaven!"

"Fine," says St. Peter, and off they go.

Heaven is a place high in the clouds, with angels drifting about, playing harps and singing. It is nice, but not as much fun as hell. Bill thinks for a quick minute and then announces his decision.

"Hmmm. I think I'd prefer hell," he tells St. Peter.

"Fine," retorts St. Peter, "as you desire."

So Bill Gates ends up in hell. Two weeks later, St. Peter decides to check on the late billionaire to see how he is doing in hell. When he gets there, he finds Bill shackled to a wall, screaming among hot flames in dark caves, being burned and tortured by demons.

"How's everything going?" he asks Bill.

Bill responds, his voice filled with anguish and disappointment, "This is awful! This is nothing like the hell I visited two weeks ago! I can't believe this is happening! What happened to that other place, with the beautiful beaches and the pretty women playing in the water?!"

"That was the demo," replies St. Peter.

A zero and an eight are walking down the street.

The zero turns to the eight and says, "Hey, why have you got your belt pulled so tight?"

Q: Why did the computer squeak?

A: Because someone stepped on its mouse.

A Russian, an American and a blonde get to talking.

The Russian says, "We were the first in space."

The American says, "We were the first on the moon!"

The blonde says, "So what. We're going to be the first to be on the sun!"

Cloning is the sincerest form of flattery.

"You can't land on the sun, you crazy person," says the Russian. "You'll burn up."

The blonde replies, "Duhhh! We're going at night!"

*I put tape on the mirrors in my house so I don't accidentally walk through into another dimension.*

–Steven Wright

When NASA first started sending astronauts into space, they quickly discovered that ballpoint pens would not work in zero gravity. So to fix the problem, NASA scientists spent decades and $12 billion to develop a pen that could write in the vacuum of space. The Russians just used a pencil.

The world's first fully computerized airliner is ready for its first flight without pilots or a crew. The plane taxies to the loading area automatically, its doors open automatically, the steps come out automatically. The passengers board the plane and take their seats. The steps retreat automatically, the doors close and the airplane taxis toward the runway.

"Good afternoon, ladies and gentlemen," a voice intones. "Welcome to the debut of the world's first fully computerized airliner. Everything on this aircraft is run electronically. Just sit back and relax. Nothing can go wrong...nothing can go wrong...nothing can go wrong..."

A helicopter is flying above Seattle when an electrical malfunction disables all of the aircraft's electronic navigation and communication equipment. Because of the clouds and haze, the pilot can't determine his position or even a course to get to the airport. The pilot sees a tall building, flies toward it, circles it, then draws a handwritten sign and holds it in the helicopter's window.

The sign says, "WHERE AM I?" in large letters.

People in the tall building quickly respond to the aircraft, draw a large sign and hold it against the building window. Their sign says, "YOU ARE IN A HELICOPTER."

The pilot smiles, waves, looks at his map and determines the course to steer to the Seattle airport and land safely.

After the helicopter lands, the co-pilot asks the pilot how the "YOU ARE IN A HELICOPTER" sign helped determine their position

The pilot responds, "I knew that had to be the Microsoft building because they gave me a technically correct but completely useless reply."

One day, Jesus and the Devil are both working at their computers. Jesus is typing away in heaven. The Devil is typing away in hell. Suddenly, a huge blackout occurs in heaven and in hell. When the lights come back on, Jesus picks up right where he left off, but the Devil's screen is still black.

Q:  What is a computer's favourite dance?

A:  Disk-o.

Satan says, "How could this happen? I did everything Jesus did!"

Then one person in hell says, "No, Jesus Saves."

When Albert Einstein is making the rounds of the speaker's circuit, he usually finds himself eagerly longing to get back to his laboratory work. One night as they are driving to yet another dinner, Einstein mentions to his chauffeur (a man who somewhat resembles Einstein in looks and manner) that he is tired of making speeches.

"I have an idea, boss," says his chauffeur. "I've heard you give this speech so many times that I bet I could give it for you."

Einstein laughs loudly and says, "Why not? Let's do it!"

When they arrive at the dinner, Einstein puts on the chauffeur's cap and jacket and sits in the back of the room. The chauffeur gives a beautiful rendition of Einstein's speech and even answers a few questions expertly. Then, a supremely pompous professor asks an extremely difficult question about antimatter formation.

Without missing a beat, the chauffeur stares at the professor and says, "Sir, the answer to that question is so simple that I will let my chauffeur, who is sitting in the back, answer it for me."

A neutron walks into a restaurant and asks, "How much for a Coke?"

The waitress says, "For you? No charge."

The teacher asks, "What is the chemical formula for water?"

Little Johnny replies, "HIJKLMNO!!"

The teacher, puzzled, asks, "What on Earth are you talking about?"

Little Johnny replies, "Yesterday you said it was H to O!"

# Ten Reasons Why TV
# Is Better Than the Internet

1. It doesn't take minutes to build the picture when you change TV channels.

2. When was the last time you tuned in to *The Simpsons* and got a "Not Found 404" message?

3. There are fewer grating colour schemes on TV—even on MTV.

4. The family never argues over which website to visit.

5. A remote control has fewer buttons than a keyboard.

6. Even the worst TV shows never excuse themselves with an "Under Construction" sign.

7. *CSI* never slows down when a lot of people tune in.

8. You just can't find those cool infomercials on the Internet.

9. Set-top boxes don't beep and whine when you hook up to cable.

10. You can't surf the Web from a couch with a pop in one hand and chips in the other.

## Table of Elements

C = carbon

Ho = holmium

Co = cobalt

La = lanthanum

Te = tellurium

CHoCoLaTe = Better living through chemistry!

Nancy decides to introduce her elderly mother to the magic of the Internet. Nancy's first move is to access the popular "Ask.com" website, and she tells her mother that it can answer any question.

Nancy's mother is very sceptical until Nancy says, "It's true, Mom. Think of something to ask it."

As Nancy sits with fingers poised over the keyboard, Nancy's mother thinks a minute, then says, "How is Aunt Helen feeling?"

Q: What can you do in radiation-contaminated rivers?

A: Nuclear fission.

A technical support person works for a 24/7 call centre. One day, he gets a call from an individual who asks what hours the call centre is open. The support worker says, "The number you dialled is open 24 hours a day, seven days a week." The caller responds, "Is that Eastern or Pacific time?"

# Old People Calling Tech Support for the Internet

- I'd like to buy the Internet. Do you know how much it is?

- Can you copy the Internet for me on this diskette?

- I would like an Internet, please.

- I just got your Internet in the mail today...

- I just downloaded the Internet. How do I use it?

- I don't have a computer at home. Is the Internet available in book form?

- Will the Internet be open on Christmas Day tomorrow?

- We're getting an Internet from you. Are you guys having any problems sending out your Internets?

- The Internet is running too slow. Could you reboot it, please?

- We're going on holiday for three months, can you suspend the Internet for us, please?

- I have a problem with my Internet. Anyone know how to get the screen smaller?

- What do you mean I have to pay for Internet access?

- I lost my Internet. I switched my computer off last night and turned it on this morning, and the internet's gone. Can you send me another one?

- The Internet site's giving me a busy signal!

A mother is teaching her three-year-old daughter, Caitlin, the Lord's Prayer. For several evenings at bedtime, Caitlin repeats after her mother the lines from the prayer. Finally, Catlin decides to go solo. The mother listens with pride as Caitlin carefully enunciates each word, right up to the end of the prayer: "Lead us not into temptation," she prays, "but deliver us some e-mail. Amen."

> It was recently discovered that research causes cancer in rats.

Tech: Hello, Friendly Internet. May I help you?

Customer: Oh, hello, young man. I was wondering if you offer online banking?

Tech: We're an Internet service provider, ma'am. You can certainly use our service to connect to online banking.

Customer: What do I need to do that?

Tech: You just need the modem in your computer. That plugs into a phone jack. Sign up for an account, and sign up for online banking with your bank.

Customer: But where does the money come out?

Tech: I'm not sure I understand?

Customer: You know…does the money come out from that slot on the computer?

A salesman for a mobile home dealership receives call from a customer who is having problems with her air conditioner.

She says, "Mr. X, we are about to freeze to death! I keep turning the AC down, but it won't go off!"

In the beginning was the computer.
And God said, "Let there be light!"
# You have not signed on yet.
God types in his User Password: Omniscient.
# Password Incorrect. Try again!
God types: Omnipotent.
# Password Incorrect. Try again!

Eventually, Bill Gates croaks, and Satan is there to greet him. "Welcome, Mr. Gates, we've been waiting for you. This will be your home for all eternity. You've been selfish, greedy and a big liar all your life. Now, since you've caught me in a good mood, I'll be generous and give you a choice of three places in which you'll be locked up forever."

The first place Satan takes Bill to is a huge lake of fire in which millions of poor souls are tormented and tortured. He then takes him to a massive coliseum where thousands of people are chased about and devoured by starving lions. Finally, he takes Bill to a tiny room in which there is a beautiful young blonde with a big smile on her face, sitting at a table on which there is a bottle of the finest wine.

To Bill's delight, he sees a computer in the corner. Without hesitation, Bill says, "I'll take this option!"

> I wondered why the baseball kept getting bigger. Then it hit me.

"Fine," says Satan, allowing Bill to enter the room. Satan locks the room after Bill. As Satan turns around, he bumps into Lucifer.

"That was Bill Gates!" cries Lucifer. "Why did you give him the best place of all?"

"That's what everyone thinks," snickers Satan. "The bottle has a hole in it, and the girl hates him!"

"What about the PC?"

"It's got Windows XP!" laughs Satan. "And it's missing three keys."

"Which three?"

"Control, Alt and Delete."

One night, an Air Canada plane is flying somewhere above Toronto. There are five people on board: the pilot, Wayne Gretzky, Bill Gates, the Dalai Lama and a hippie.

Suddenly, an illegal oxygen generator explodes in the luggage compartment, and the passenger cabin begins to fill with smoke. The cockpit door opens, and the pilot comes running out.

"Gentlemen," he says, "I have good news and bad news. The bad news is that we're about to crash in Toronto. The good news is that there are four parachutes, and I have one of them!" With that, the pilot throws open the door and jumps from the plane.

Wayne Gretzky is on his feet in a flash. "Gentlemen," he says, "I am the world's greatest athlete. The world needs great athletes. I think the world's greatest athlete should have a parachute!" With those words, he grabs one of the remaining parachutes and hurls himself through the door and into the night.

Bill Gates rises and says, "Gentlemen, I am the world's smartest man. The world needs smart men. I think the world's smartest man should have a parachute, too." He grabs one and jumps out.

The Dalai Lama and the hippie look at one another. Finally, the Dalai Lama speaks. "My son," he says to the hippie, "I have lived a satisfying life and have known the bliss of True Enlightenment. You have your life ahead of you, so you take the parachute, and I will go down with the plane."

The hippie smiles slowly and says, "Hey, don't worry, Pop. The world's smartest man just jumped out wearing my backpack."

Stephen Harper, David Suzuki and Bill Gates all die in a plane crash and go to meet their maker.

The supreme deity turns to Suzuki and says, "Tell me, what is important about yourself?"

. Suzuki responds that he feels that the earth is of the ultimate importance and that protecting the earth's ecological system is most important.

God looks at Suzuki and says, "I like the way you think. Come and sit at my left hand."

God then asks Harper what he reveres most. Harper responds that he believes people and their personal choices are most important.

God responds, "I like the way you think. Come and sit at my right hand."

God then turns to Bill Gates, who is staring at him angrily. God asks, "What's your problem?

Bill Gates responds, "You're sitting in my chair."

## CHAPTER TEN

# Pets, Piranhas and Pachyderms

A woman famous for her charitable work is granted three wishes by a fairy godmother.

"I have everything I could possibly want in life. What more can I wish for?" She ponders for a moment and says, "I could use a new sofa. I've had this one for 30 years."

With a wave of her wand, the fairy godmother turns the old couch into a brand new suede sofa.

"Now, what is your second wish?"

"Really, I can't imagine what I would need. Well, I could use a new car to get me to work."

The fairy godmother waves her wand again, and a brand new car appears in her driveway.

Q: What did the idiot call his pet zebra?

A: Spot!

"And now for your third and final wish."

"Well, I have never married, and it would be nice to have someone to share these wonderful things with. Could you turn my cat into a handsome leading man?"

With another wave of the fairy godmother's wand, the cat is turned into a handsome hunk.

The handsome young man then says, "I bet you're sorry you had me neutered now!"

Two fleas are planning a trip to the far side of a house.

One turns to the other and says, "Shall we hop or take the cat?"

A third-grade class is completing a writing exercise, and Donny asks the teacher how to spell "piranha." The teacher tells Donny that she isn't sure. To the teacher's delight, Donny goes to the dictionary to solve his problem. That's when the teacher overhears another student say to Donny, "Why bother to look it up? She doesn't know how to spell it anyway."

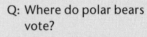

Q: Where do polar bears vote?

A: The North Poll.

Q: What do you get when you cross an elephant with a spider?

A: I'm not sure, but if you see one, RUN!

*I once shot an elephant in my pajamas. How he got into my pajamas, I'll never know.*

—Groucho Marx

A father spots his four-year-old son out in the backyard, brushing the family dog's teeth.

"What are you doing?" screams the father.

"I'm brushing Rover's teeth," says the little boy. "But don't worry, Daddy, I'll put your toothbrush back like I always do."

A girl and her mother walk into the local veterinarian's office to pick up their dog.

The vet comes in carrying the dog and says with a strained voice: "I'm afraid I have to put your dog down."

The young girl bursts into tears and screams, "Why?"

"Because he's too heavy."

Q: What's the red stuff between an elephant's toes?
A: Slow tourists.

Q: What's the difference between an elephant and a flea?
A: An elephant can have fleas, but a flea cannot have elephants.

A little girl walks into a pet store and asks for a nice warm sweater for her dog. The sales assistant suggests it would be better to bring the dog in to make sure the sweater will fit.

With a confused look on her face, the little girl replies, "I can't do that! The sweater is a surprise!"

Two dogs are walking down the street when one suddenly sniffs the air and crosses the street. For about a minute, the dog sniffs around a lamppost and fire hydrant then crosses back again.

"What was that about?" asks the other dog.

"Just checking my messages."

A boy goes over to his friend's house to show off his new dog and the amazing tricks he's taught it.

"I'll bet you your Xbox that my dog can talk," says the proud boy.

His friend takes him up on the challenge.

The boy looks at his dog and asks, "What is on top of this building to prevent the rain from running in?"

The dog answers, "Roof."

> Q: Where do rabbits go after their wedding?
>
> A: On their bunnymoon.
>
> Q: What do you give a sick bird?
>
> A: Tweetment.

"I'm not falling for this!" says the boy's friend.

"Okay," says the boy. "How about I get him to say something else. Who was the greatest baseball player of all time?"

The dog answers, "Roof."

"Alright," says the friend. "Get out of my house. I don't have time for your games."

As they walked back to their house, the dog looks up at his master and says, "Should I have said Bonds?"

*I gave my cat a bath the other day. They love it. He just sat there and enjoyed it. It was fun for me. The fur kept sticking to my tongue, but other than that...*

–Steve Martin

## The Magician and the Parrot

A magician is working on a cruise ship in the Caribbean. The audience is different each week, so the magician allows himself to do the same tricks over and over again.

There is only one problem: the captain's parrot has seen the show every week and begins to understand what the magician does in every trick, so he starts shouting in the middle of the show. "Look, it's not the same hat!" "Look, he's hiding the flowers under the table!" "Hey, why are all the cards the ace of spades?"

The magician is furious but can't do anything; it is the captain's parrot, after all. One day, the ship has an accident and sinks. The magician finds himself floating on a piece of wood in the middle of the ocean, and of course, the parrot is by his side. They stare at each other with hate but do not utter a word. This goes on for several days.

Q: How do you know carrots are good for your eyes?

A: Because you never see rabbits wearing glasses!

☺☺

Q: What is a bunny's motto?

A: "Don't be mad, be hoppy!"

After a week, the parrot finally says, "Okay, I give up. What'd you do with the boat?"

## City Girl

A young woman from Toronto visits a farm for the first time and asks the farmer, "Mister, why doesn't this cow have any horns?"

The farmer cocks his head for a moment and then says in a patient tone, "Well, ma'am, cattle can do a powerful lot of damage with horns. Sometimes we trim the horns with a hacksaw. Other times we put a few drops of acid where their horns would grow in, and that stops 'em cold. Still, there are some breeds of cattle that never grow horns. But the reason this cow don't have no horns, ma'am, is 'cause it's a horse."

Two boys with dogs are arguing about which of their dogs is smarter.

First boy: "My dog is so smart that every morning he waits for the paper boy to come, then he picks up the newspaper and brings it to me.

Second boy: "I know…"

First boy: "How?"

Second boy: "My dog told me."

Q: Why do bees hum?

A: Because they don't know the words.

Q: What did the idiot do to the flea in his ear?

A: He shot it.

## Three Signs Your Cat Is Trying to Kill You

1. You wake up and find a bird head on your pillow.

2. He takes notes whenever *Itchy and Scratchy* is on.

3. He quietly stares at you while sharpening his claws.

A boy goes to a pet shop and buys a talking parrot. He takes the parrot home and tries to teach it how to say a few words, but instead, it just swears at him.

After a few hours of trying to teach the bird, the boy finally says, "If you don't stop swearing, I'm going to put you in the freezer as punishment."

The parrot continues to swear, so the boy puts it in the freezer.

About an hour later, the parrot asks the boy to please open the door.

As the boy is taking the shivering bird out of the freezer, the parrot says, "I promise never to swear again. Just tell me what that turkey did!"

Q: What is a rabbit's favourite dance style?

A: Hip-Hop.

A shy young man ventures into a coffee shop in the city and, clearing his throat, asks, "Um, err, which of you gentlemen owns the doberman tied outside to the parking meter?"

A giant of a man, wearing biker leathers and body hair growing out through the seams, turns slowly on his stool, looks down at the quivering little man and says, "It's my dog. Why?"

"Well," squeaked the little man, obviously very nervous, "I believe my dog just killed it, sir."

"What?!" roars the big man in disbelief. "What in the hell kind of dog do you have?"

"Sir," answers the little man, "it's a little four-week-old female puppy."

"Bull!" roars the biker, "how could your puppy kill my doberman?"

Q: Why aren't dogs good dancers?

A: Because they have two left feet.

"It appears that your dog choked on her, sir."

A cowboy rides into town and goes into the saloon for a few drinks. When he comes out again, his horse is gone.

He storms back into the saloon and shouts, "Who stole my horse?"

No one says anything.

Getting increasingly frustrated he says, "Right, if no one owns up to stealing my horse, I'm going to do what I did in Texas."

Still silence.

"This is your last chance. If no one comes forward with my horse, I am going to do what I did in Texas."

Then one lone voice speaks up, "What did you do in Texas?"

The cowboy replies, "I walked home."

Billy's mother walks into the kitchen to find him stalking around with a fly swatter.

"Have you killed any?" she asks.

"Yep," replies Billy. "Three males and two females."

"How can you tell?" she asks.

"Three were on a beer can, and two were on the phone."

Q: What did the judge say when the skunk walked in the court room?

A: Odour in the court!

Little Tim is in the garden filling a hole when his older neighbour, Tom, peers over the fence. Interested in what the youngster is doing, Tom politely asks, "What are you up to there, Tim?"

"My goldfish died," replies Tim tearfully, without looking up, "and I've just buried him."

Tom says, "That's an awfully big hole for a goldfish, isn't it, Tim?"

Tim pats down the last heap of earth and replies, "That's because I couldn't get him out of your cat."

A postal worker is delivering mail one day and meets a boy and a dog.

"Does your dog bite?" she asks the boy.

"No," replies the boy. And the dog bites the postal worker's leg.

"You said he didn't bite!" screams the woman.

"That's not my dog," replies the boy.

> Q: What is the difference between a fish and a piano?
> A: You can't tuna fish.

A dog is sitting in a theatre with its owner. The dog stares at the screen intently and growls whenever the villain appears on screen, and it wags its tail whenever the hero comes on. A woman sitting nearby is watching the dog's behaviour.

"That's incredible behaviour for a dog," she says.

> Q: What kind of bird works at a construction site?
> A: The crane.

"You're right," says the owner. "It's surprising because he hated the book."

A man enters a little country store in Alberta and reads a sign: "Danger! Beware of Dog." He then sees an old hound sleeping on the floor.

"Is that the dog folks are supposed to beware of?" says the man to the clerk.

"Yep," replies the clerk. "Before I posted that sign, everyone kept tripping over him."

A boy sees a sign in front of a house that reads: "Talking Dog for Sale." Interested, the boy rings the doorbell and the owner takes him to the backyard, where the dog is chained to a post.

Q: What do you call two elephants on a bicycle?

A: Optimistic.

"Can you talk?" asks the boy.

"Sure can," says the dog. "I discovered this gift when I was young. I decided to help the government, so I got in touch with the CIA. In no time they had me jetting from country to country, sitting in rooms with spies and world leaders, because no one would think a dog would be listening to their conversations. I was one of their most valuable spies for eight years. But all that work made me tired, and I wanted to settle down. So I signed up for a job at the airport to do some undercover security work, mostly just wandering near suspicious characters and listening in. I uncovered some crazy things and was awarded a few medals for my work. Later I found a wife, had some puppies and now I'm retired. It's been a crazy life."

The little boy is amazed. He asks the owner how much he wants for the dog.

"Ten dollars," replies the owner.

"That's it?! For such an amazing dog?" says the boy. "Why would you be selling such an incredible dog?"

The owner replies, "Because he's such a big liar!"

Q: What is invisible and smells like carrots?

A: Bunny farts.

Q: Why does a flamingo lift up one leg?

A: Because if it lifted both legs, it would fall over.

A man walks by a table in a casino and sees three men and a dog playing poker.

"That's an amazing dog," says the man.

"He's not so clever," says one of the players. "Every time he gets a good hand, he wags his tail."

A rabbit walks into a restaurant with a lion. The waiter seats them and asks the rabbit, "What will you have?"

The rabbit orders half a head of lettuce.

The waiter looks at the lion and says to the rabbit, "And what will he have?"

Q: What do bulls do when they go shopping?

A: They CHARGE!

The rabbit says, "The lion? He's not eating."

The waiter says, "Why? Isn't he hungry?"

The rabbit says, "If he was hungry, do you think I'd be here?"

Joe lost his dog and didn't know what to do, so he put an ad in the newspaper that read: "Here, boy!"

Q: What do you call a dog with no legs?

A: It doesn't matter, he still won't come.

A dog goes into a grocery store with a basket in his mouth. In the basket is a shopping list and a purse. The grocer reads the list, puts the items in the basket, takes the money out of the purse and puts the receipt in the basket. The dog then leaves the store and runs back home. This happens every week for over a month. One day, the grocer decides to follow the dog home and ask the owner how he taught the dog such amazing things. He follows the dog, and it eventually leads him to a rundown house where it puts down the basket on the doorstep and rings the doorbell with its nose. After a few seconds, an old woman opens the door and starts yelling at the dog and hits it with a stick.

"Stop that!" shouts the grocer. "What are you doing? That's the most intelligent dog I've ever seen in my life."

"Intelligent? Ha!" laughs the old lady. "That's the third time this week he's forgotten his keys."

> Q: What's small, cuddly and bright purple?
> A: A koala holding its breath.
>
> Q: What is the difference between a flea and a wolf?
> A: One prowls on the hairy and the other howls on the prairie.

A dog goes into an employment agency and asks for a job.

"Wow, a talking dog," says the clerk. "With your talent, I'm sure we can find you a job with the circus."

"The circus?" says the dog. "What would the circus want with an accountant?"

Q: Why did the judge dismiss the jury made up entirely of cats?

A: Because each of them was guilty of purrjury.

A woman comes home from work one day and discovers that her dog is not moving. She takes it to a vet who, after a brief examination, announces that the dog is dead.

"Are you sure?" the woman asks. "Isn't there the slightest chance you can revive him?"

The vet thinks for a second, then leaves the room and comes back with a cat. The cat walks over to the dog, sniffs it from head to foot, looks at the vet and shakes its head.

"I'm sorry," says the vet. "Your dog is definitely dead."

Satisfied that the vet has done everything possible, the woman asks for his bill.

"That will be $1500," the vet replies.

The woman is astonished. "I don't believe it," she says. "What did you do that cost so much?"

"Well," replies the vet, "it's $100 for the visit, $100 for supplies and $1300 for a CAT scan."

*Is a hippopotamus really a hippopotamus or just a really cool opotomus?*

–Mitch Hedberg, comedian

A sloth is walking through the jungle one day when a gang of vicious snails attacks him.

The snails leave the sloth bleeding and confused at the bottom of a tree. Several hours later, the sloth summons the strength to go to the police station to report the assault. The desk sergeant asks him to describe his attackers.

The sloth replies, "I don't know what they looked like. It all happened so fast…"

An out-of-towner accidentally drives his car into a deep ditch beside a country road. Luckily, a farmer happens by with his big old horse named Benny. The man asks the farmer for help. The farmer tells him that Benny can pull his car out.

He backs Benny up and hitches him to the man's car bumper and yells, "Pull, Nellie, pull!"

> Q: Why are igloos round?
> A: So polar bears can't hide in the corners.

Benny doesn't move.

Then the farmer yells, "Come on, pull, Ranger!"

Still, Benny doesn't move.

Then he yells really loud, "Now pull, Fred, pull hard!"

Benny just stands there.

Then the farmer nonchalantly says, "Okay, Benny, pull."

Benny easily pulls the car out of the ditch. The man is very appreciative but curious. He asks the farmer why he called his horse by the wrong name three times.

The farmer says, "Oh, Benny is blind, and if he thought he was the only one pulling, he wouldn't even try."

Q: What do you get if you cross a fish with an elephant?

A: Swimming trunks.

A duck walks into a convenience store and asks the clerk, "Do you have any grapes?"

The clerk says no, and the duck leaves.

The next day, the duck returns and asks, "Do you have any grapes?"

The clerk again says no, and the duck leaves.

The day after that, the duck walks in the store again and asks, "Do you have any grapes?"

The clerk screams at the duck, "You've come in here the past two days and asked if we have any grapes. Every day I tell you 'no, we don't have any grapes'! I swear, if you come back in here again and ask for grapes, I'll nail your webbed feet to the floor!"

The duck leaves and returns the next day.

This time he asks, "Do you have any nails?"

The clerk replies, "No."

The duck says, "Good! Got any grapes?"

A married couple is going out for the evening and calls a taxi. The last thing they do before leaving is put the cat outside.

The taxi arrives, and as the couple walk out of the house, the cat runs back inside. So, the husband goes back in to chase her out.

The wife, not wanting it known that the house will be empty, explains to the taxi driver "He's just going upstairs to say goodbye to my mother."

> Q: What's the difference between an injured lion and a wet day?
>
> A: One pours with rain, the other roars with pain.

A few minutes later, the husband gets into the taxi and says, "Sorry I took so long, the stupid thing was hiding under the bed, and I had to poke her with a coat hanger to get her to come out!"

A famous art collector is walking through Vancouver when he notices a mangy cat lapping milk from a saucer in the doorway of a store. He does a double take.

He knows that the saucer is extremely old and very valuable, so he walks casually into the store and offers to buy the cat for two dollars.

The storeowner replies, "I'm sorry, but the cat isn't for sale."

The collector says, "Please, I need a hungry cat around the house to catch mice. I'll pay you 20 dollars for that cat."

The owner says, "Sold," and hands over the cat.

The collector continues, "Hey, for the 20 bucks, I wonder if you could throw in that old saucer. The cat's used to it, and it'll save me from having to get a dish."

> Q: What do you call a gorilla wearing earmuffs?
>
> A: Anything you like. He can't hear you.

The owner says, "Sorry, buddy, but that's my lucky saucer. So far this week, I've sold 68 cats."

A mother mouse and a baby mouse are walking along, when all of a sudden, a cat attacks them.

The mother mouse screams, "WOOF!" and the cat runs away.

"See?" says the mother mouse to her baby. "Now do you see why it's important to learn a foreign language?"

A zookeeper sees a visitor throwing five-dollar bills into the monkey cage.

"What are you doing that for?" asks the keeper.

"The sign says it's okay," replies the visitor.

"No, it doesn't," replies the keeper.

"Yes, it does," says the visitor. "It says, 'Do not feed. $5 fine.'"

John hears that a zoo has managed to train a lion to live in the same cage as a lamb. He pays a visit and finds that the two animals are indeed sitting next to each other in a cage.

John approaches the zookeeper in charge. "That's incredible," says John. "How do you manage it?"

"Well, it hasn't been easy," says the keeper. "And most mornings we do have to buy a new lamb."

A man is at the zoo and asks the keeper, "Do you have any talking parrots?"

"No," says the keeper, "but we have a woodpecker that knows Morse code."

A leopard keeps trying to escape from the zoo, but he is never successful. He is always spotted.

# A Dog's Rules for Christmas

1. Be especially patient with your humans during this time. They may appear to be more stressed-out than usual, and they will appreciate long, comforting dog cuddles.

2. They may come home with large bags of things they call gifts. Do not assume all the gifts are yours.

3. Be tolerant if your humans put decorations on you. They seem to get some special kind of pleasure out of seeing how you look with fake antlers.

4. They may bring a large tree into the house, set it up in a prominent place and cover it with lights and decorations. Bizarre as this may seem to you, it's an important ritual for humans, so there are some things you need to know:

    a. Don't pee on the tree.

    b. Don't drink the water in the container that holds the tree.

    c. Mind your tail when you are near the tree.

    d. If there are packages under the tree, even ones that smell interesting or that have your name on them, don't rip them open.

    e. Don't chew on the cord that runs from the funny-looking hole in the wall to the tree.

5. Your humans may occasionally invite a lot of strangers to come visit during this season. These parties can be fun, but they also call for some discretion on your part:

    a. Not all strangers appreciate kisses.

    b. Don't eat off the buffet table.

    c. Beg for goodies subtly.

    d. Be pleasant, even if unknowing strangers sit on your sofa.

    e. Don't drink out of glasses that are left within your reach.

6. Likewise, your humans may take you visiting. Here, your manners are even more important:

    a. Observe all the rules in #4 for trees that may be in other people's houses (4a is particularly important).

    b. Respect the territory of other animals that may live in the house.

    c. Tolerate children.

    d. Turn on the charm big time.

7. A big man with a white beard and a very loud laugh may emerge from your fireplace in the middle of the night. DON'T BITE HIM!

A father and his small son are standing in front of the tiger's cage at the zoo. The father explains to his son how ferocious and strong tigers are, and the boy is taking it all very seriously.

In the end, the little boy asks, "Dad, just one question. If the tiger gets out of his cage and eats you up, which bus do I take home?"

Marvin's mother is very hard to please, but one year he thinks hard and finally comes up with a truly inspired birthday present: a gorgeous parrot that speaks six languages. He pays a lot of money for the parrot and arranges to have the bird in a fancy antique cage delivered to her apartment on the day of her birthday.

That evening, he visits his mother for her birthday dinner.

"So, Mom, did you get my present?" he asks.

"Yes, Marvin, I did. And I must say, it cooked up very nicely."

"You didn't cook it!" gasps Marvin. "Mom, that bird cost me $1500. And it spoke English, Spanish, French, Mandarin, Russian and Polish!"

"Now, Marvin," the old woman chides, "if it really spoke all those languages, why didn't it say something?"

## CHAPTER ELEVEN

# Growing Pains

Teenager to father: "How can you expect me to be independent, self-reliant and stand on my own two feet on the tiny allowance you give me?"

You know you are growing up when you stop asking your parents where you came from and stop telling them where you are going.

Why do teenagers say they're not like anyone else and then all dress exactly alike?

Rick has just received his brand new driver's licence. The family troops out to the driveway and climbs into the car, because he is going to take them for a ride for the first time. Dad immediately heads for the back seat, directly behind the newly-minted driver.

"I'll bet you're back there to get a change of scenery after all those months of sitting in the front passenger seat teaching me how to drive," says the beaming boy to his father.

"Nope," comes the dad's reply, "I'm gonna sit here and kick the back of your seat as you drive, just like you've been doing to me all these years."

An army brat is boasting about his father to a navy brat.

"My dad is an engineer. He can do everything. Do you know the Alps?"

"Yes," says the navy brat.

"My dad built them."

The navy kid then says, "And do you know the Dead Sea?"

"Yes."

"It was my dad who killed it!"

An eight-year-old boy goes into a grocery store and picks out a large box of laundry detergent. A grocery clerk walks over and asks the boy if he has a lot of laundry to do.

"Oh, no laundry," says the boy. "I'm going to wash my dog."

"But you shouldn't use this to wash your dog," says the clerk. "It's very powerful, and if you wash your dog in this, he'll get sick. In fact, it might even kill him."

But the boy doesn't listen and carries the detergent to the counter and pays for it.

A week later, the boy is back in the store to buy some candy. The same grocery clerk asks the boy how his dog is doing.

"Oh, he died," says the boy.

The clerk says he is sorry, but adds, "I tried to tell you not to use that detergent on your dog."

"Well," replies the boy, "I don't think it was the detergent that killed him."

"Oh? What was it then?"

"I think it was the spin cycle."

While proudly showing off his new apartment to friends after a night on the town, a college student leads the way into the den.

"What is the big brass gong and hammer for?" one of his friends asks.

"That is the talking clock," the young man replies.

"How does it work?"

"Watch," says the man and proceeds to give the gong an ear-shattering pound with the hammer.

Suddenly, someone screams from the other side of the wall, "Knock it off, you idiot! It's two o'clock in the morning!"

# A Teenager Is...

A person who can't remember to walk the dog but never forgets a phone number.

A weight watcher who goes on a diet by giving up candy bars before breakfast.

A youngster who receives his allowance on Monday, spends it on Tuesday and borrows from his best friend on Wednesday.

Someone who can hear a song by Nickelback played three blocks away but not his mother calling from the next room.

A whiz who can operate the latest computer without a lesson but can't make a bed.

A student who will spend 12 minutes studying for her history exam and 12 hours for her driver's licence.

A youngster who is well informed about anything he doesn't have to study.

An enthusiast who has the energy to ride a bike for miles but is usually too tired to dry the dishes.

A connoisseur of two kinds of fine music: Loud and Very Loud.

A young woman who loves the cat and tolerates her brother.

A person who is always late for dinner but always on time for a rock concert.

A romantic who never falls in love more than once a week.

A mother and father have just given their teen-age daughter permission to drive the family car. On Saturday night, she returns home very late from a party.

The next morning, her father goes out to the driveway to get the newspaper and comes back into the house, frowning. At 11:30 AM, the girl sleepily walks into the kitchen.

Her father asks her, "Sweetheart, what time did you get in last night?"

"Not too late, Dad," she replies, nervously.

With a serious look on his face, her father says, "Then, my precious one, I'll have to talk with the paperboy about putting my newspaper under the front tire of the car."

"Honey, I think our daughter wants to be an actress," says a woman to her husband.

"Don't worry, dear," replies the husband. "It's just a stage she's going through."

A young man has just received his driver's licence. He asks his father, who is a minister, if they can discuss his use of the car.

His father says to him, "I'll make a deal with you. You bring your grades up, study the Bible a bit and get your hair cut, and then we will talk about it."

A month later, the boy comes back and again asks his father if they can discuss his use of the car.

His father says, "Son, I'm real proud of you. You've brought your grades up and studied the Bible diligently, but you didn't get your hair cut!"

The young man waits a moment and then replies, "You know, Dad, I've been thinking about that. Samson had long hair, Moses had long hair, Noah had long hair, and even Jesus had long hair."

His father replies, "Yes, son, and they all walked everywhere they went!"

One night, a teenage girl in Montreal brings her new boyfriend home to meet her parents. They are appalled by his appearance: leather jacket, motorcycle boots, tattoos and a pierced nose. Later, the parents pull their daughter aside and confess their concern.

"Dear," says the mother diplomatically, "he doesn't seem very nice."

"Oh please, Mom," replies the daughter, "if he wasn't nice, why would he be doing 500 hours of community service?"

Having moved into his first apartment, a young man invites his parents over for a visit.

As they walk in, the son asks if they'd like a cold drink.

The mother, mentally patting herself on the back for teaching her son to be such a gracious host, says, "Yes, what do you have?"

The young man walks over to the refrigerator, opens the door, studies the contents and then replies, "I have pickle juice or water."

## Pizza Delivery Job

A high school kid on his first day of his new pizza delivery job makes a delivery to an old man's house.

"I suppose you want a tip?" replies the grumpy old man.

"That would be great," says the high school kid, "but the other guy who does deliveries told me not to expect much from you. He said if I got a quarter from you, I'd be lucky."

Hurt by the accusation, the old man says, "Well, to prove him wrong, here's five dollars."

"Thank you," says the high school student, "I'll put this in my college fund."

"What do you want to study?" asks the old man.

"Applied psychology."

It's "Bring Your Parent to School" day at a local high school. One father is sitting beside his son in chemistry class, and his son shows him one of the experiments they are conducting in order to find a universal solvent.

"What's that?" asks the confused father.

"It's a liquid that will dissolve anything," replies his son.

"It sounds good," says the father. "But when you find it, what kind of container will you keep it in?"

## Choose Wisely

A graduate with a science degree asks: "Why does it work?"

A graduate with an engineering degree asks, "How does it work?"

A graduate with an accounting degree asks: "How much does it cost?"

A graduate with an arts degree asks: "Do you want fries with that?"

A little girl goes to her local library to take out a book called *Advice for Young Mothers*.

"Why do you want to take out a book like that?" asks the librarian.

"Because I collect moths."

Mark is 5 feet, 8 inches tall when he leaves for college in the fall. He works through the Christmas holidays and doesn't return home again until spring break.

When he gets off the plane, his mother is stunned at how much taller he looks. Measuring him at home, she discovers he is now 5 feet, 11 inches. Mark is as surprised as his mother.

"Couldn't you tell by your clothes that you'd grown?" she asks him.

"Since I've been doing my own laundry," replies Mark, "I just figured everything had shrunk."

A cop gets out of his car, and the teenager, who has been stopped for speeding, rolls down his window.

"I've been waiting for you all day," the cop says.

The kid replies, "Yeah, well, I got here as fast as I could."

When the cop finally stops laughing, he sends the kid on his way without a ticket.

## How to Handle Noisy Teens

A wise old gentleman retires and buys a modest home near a junior high school. He spends the first few weeks of his retirement in peace and contentment. Then a new school year begins.

The very next afternoon, three young boys, full of youthful, after-school enthusiasm, come down his street, beating merrily on every trashcan they encounter. The crashing percussion continues day after day, until finally the wise old man decides it is time to take action.

The next afternoon, he walks out to meet the young percussionists as they bang their way down the street. Stopping them, he says, "You kids are a lot of fun. I like to see you express your exuberance like that. In fact, I used to do the same thing when I was your age. Will you do me a favour? I'll give you each a dollar if you'll promise to come around every day and do your thing."

The kids are elated and continue to do a bang-up job on the trashcans.

After a few days, the old-timer greets the kids again, but this time he has a sad smile on his face. "This recession has really put a big dent in my income," he tells them. "From now on, I'll only be able to pay you 50 cents to beat on the cans."

The noisemakers were obviously displeased, but they accept his offer and continue their afternoon ruckus. A few days later, the wily retiree approaches them again as they drum their way down the street.

"Look," he says, "I haven't received my pension cheque yet, so I can't give you more than 25 cents. Is that okay?"

"A lousy quarter?" the drum leader exclaims. "If you think we're going to waste our time, beating these cans around for a quarter, you're nuts! No way, mister. We quit!"

And the old man enjoyed peace and quiet from then on.

A three-year-old boy goes with his dad to see a new litter of kittens. On returning home, the boy breathlessly informs his mother, "There were two boy kittens and two girl kittens."

"How do you know that?" his mother asks.

"Daddy picked them up and looked underneath," he replies. "I think it's printed on the bottom!"

As a family gathers for a big dinner together, the youngest son announces that he had just signed up at an army recruiter's office.

There are audible gasps around the table, then some laughter, as his older brothers share their disbelief that he could handle this new situation.

"Oh, come on, quit joking," snickers one. "You didn't really do that, did you?"

"You would never get through basic training," scoffs another brother.

The new recruit looks to his mother for help, but she is just gazing at him.

When she finally speaks, she asks, "Do you really plan to make your own bed every morning?"

A professor stands before his class of 20 senior organic biology students, about to hand out the final exam.

"I want to say that it has been a pleasure teaching you this semester. I know you've all worked extremely hard, and many of you are off to medical school after summer. So that no one gets their GPA messed up because they might have been celebrating a bit too much this week, anyone who would like to opt out of the final exam today will receive a 'B' for the course."

There is much rejoicing in the class as the students get up, walk to the front of the class and take the professor up on his offer. As the last taker leaves the room, the professor looks out over the handful of remaining students and asks, "Anyone else? This is your last chance."

One final student stands up and opts out of the final. The professor then closes the door and takes the attendance of the students still remaining.

"I'm glad to see you believe in yourselves," he says. "You all get 'A's."

Just as an elderly woman is turning her Mercedes into a parking space at the mall, a red Mustang edges her out and steals her parking space.

"You've got to be young and fast," laughs the teenaged driver as he jumps out of his car.

The woman reverses, revs her engine and rams the Mustang. As the Mercedes reverses and heads for the car again, the teenager runs over and bangs on the window.

"What the heck do you think you're doing?" he yells.

She smiles sweetly and explains, "Well, I'm old and rich!"

## CHAPTER TWELVE

# Weird, Wild and Wacky

A 10-year-old boy is having trouble with his math homework.

"Grandpa," he asks, "could you please help me with this?"

"I could," replies the grandfather, "but it wouldn't be right, would it?"

"I guess it wouldn't, Grandpa," says the boy, "but have a shot at it anyway."

A man comes home from work and notices that his father seems to be avoiding the grandchildren.

"What's the problem?" he asks his father. "Normally you love playing with the kids."

The old man pulls out a medicine prescription from his pocket, gives it to his son and says, "Read the label. That's why!"

The man looks at the prescription and reads the label: "Take two pills a day. KEEP AWAY FROM CHILDREN."

Q: Why did the kid put candles on the toilet?

A: He wanted to have a birthday potty!

Q: What do you call a man with no arms and no legs who is in the hot tub?

A: Stew.

# Things to Do in the Bathroom

1. Stick your open palm under the stall wall and ask your neighbour, "May I borrow a highlighter?"

2. Say: "Uh-oh, I knew I shouldn't have put my lips on that."

3. Cheer and clap loudly every time somebody breaks the silence with a bodily function noise.

4. Say: "Hmmm, I've never seen that colour before."

5. Drop a marble and say, "Oh, shoot! My glass eye!"

6. Say: "Darn, this water is cold."

7. Grunt and strain real loud for 30 seconds and then drop a cantaloupe into the toilet bowl from six to eight feet high. Sigh contentedly.

8. Say: "Now, how did that get there?"

9. Say: "Humus. Reminds me of humus."

10. Fill up a large bottle with Mountain Dew. Squirt it erratically under the stall walls of your neighbour while yelling, "Whoa! Easy boy!"

11. Say: "Interesting...more sinkers than floaters."

12. Using a small squeeze tube, spread peanut butter on a wad of toilet paper and drop it under the stall wall of your neighbour. Then say, "Whoops, could you kick that back over here, please?"

13. Say: "Darn, I knew that drain hole was a little too small. Now what am I gonna do?"

14. Lower a small mirror underneath the stall wall and adjust it so you can see your neighbour and say, "Peek-a-boo!"

15. Take a Snickers chocolate bar with you, squish it in your hand and reach under the stall wall and say, "You got any more toilet paper over there? This side's completely out."

## Crazy Things to Do in an Elevator

Make race-car noises when anyone gets on or off.

Grimace painfully while smacking your forehead and muttering: "Shut up, all of you just SHUT UP!"

Sell Girl Scout cookies.

Offer nametags to everyone getting on the elevator. Wear yours upside down.

Stand silent and motionless in the corner, facing the wall, without getting off.

When at your floor, strain to yank the doors open, then act embarrassed when they open by themselves.

Greet everyone getting on the elevator with a warm handshake and ask them to call you Admiral.

Bring a chair along.

A boy is visiting his grandmother with a friend. While the boy talks to his grandmother in the kitchen, his friend sees a bowl of peanuts on the living room table and starts to eat them.

When it's time to go, the friend calls out, "Thanks for the peanuts."

"That's okay," replies grandmother. "Since I lost my dentures, I can only suck the chocolate off them."

Mark: "Hey, what was that loud noise?"

Amar: "My jacket fell on the floor."

Mark: "Why did your jacket make such a loud noise?"

Amar: "Because I was in it when it fell!"

Two guys are out hunting deer.

The first guy says, "Did you see that?" and points to the sky.

"No," says the second guy.

"Well, a bald eagle just flew overhead!" says the first guy.

"Oh," says the second guy.

A couple of minutes later, pointing to a far ridge, the first guy says, "Did you see that?"

"See what?" the second guy asks.

"Are you blind? There was a big black bear walking on that hill, over there!"

"Yeah. Okay," says the second guy again with a bit of irritation in his voice.

A few minutes later, the first guy says, "Did you see that?" This time he points behind them.

Q: Why are there so many Johnsons in the phone book?

A: They all have phones.

Q: What do you call a guy at your front door with no legs or arms?

A: Matt.

Q: How do trumpet players traditionally greet each other?

A: Hi. I'm better than you.

By now, the second guy is getting aggravated and says, "Yeah, I SAW IT!"

And the first guy says, "Then why did you step in it?"

## Strange Questions

Is it okay to use the AM radio after noon?

What do chickens think we taste like?

What do people in China call their good plates?

What do you call a male ladybug?

What hair colour do they put on the driver's licence of a bald man?

When dog food is new and improved tasting, who tests it?

When they first invented the clock, how did they know what time it was to set it to?

Which is the other side of the street?

Why didn't Noah swat those two mosquitoes?

Why doesn't glue stick to the inside of the bottle?

Why don't they call moustaches "mouthbrows"?

If a Smurf is choking, what colour does it turn?

Is there another word for synonym?

Little Boy: "My little brother stuck his head in our washing machine."

Friend: "What happened to him?"

Little Boy: "He got brainwashed."

A big-time corporate negotiator is out fishing one day when he catches a strange-looking fish. He reels the fish in, unhooks it and throws it on the ground.

The fish starts writhing in agony and, to the man's surprise, says, "Please throw me back into the lake, and I'll grant you three wishes."

Q: What do you get when you cross a motorcycle and a joke?

A: A Yama ha-ha!

"Any three wishes, huh?" The negotiator thinks of all the expensive cars that he could suddenly have.

"Fish," he finally says, "give me *five* wishes, and I'll throw you back."

"Sorry," answers the fish while struggling for breath, "only three wishes."

The negotiator's pride is at stake, and after giving the matter some thought, he says, "What do you take me for? A sucker? I'll settle for *four* wishes."

The Energizer Bunny is arrested; he is charged with battery.

"Only three," whispers the fish, weakly.

Fuming, the man debates the pros and cons of accepting the three wishes or continuing to bargain for that one extra wish. Finally, the man decides it isn't worth bargaining and says, "All right, fish, you win, three wishes."

Unfortunately, the fish dies.

*People can come up with statistics to prove anything. Fourteen percent of people know that.*

—Homer Simpson

A man with two left feet walks into a shoe store and says, "Got any flip-flips?"

Sam isn't happy about putting his dad in a nursing home, but it's all he can afford—until a lucky investment pays off. The first thing he does with his newfound wealth is move his father to the best nursing home available.

The old man is astounded by the luxury of his new surroundings. On the first day, as he is sitting in front of the television, he starts to lean to his right side. Instantly, a nurse runs over and straightens him out. Over lunch, he starts to lean a bit to the left, but

Q:  What did the big chimney say to the little chimney?

A:  You're too young to smoke.

within a few seconds a nurse gently pushes him upright again.

That night, his son calls and says, "How are you doing, Pop?"

"Oh, Sam, it's a wonderful place," replies the father. "I've got my own colour TV, the food is cooked by a French chef, the gardens are beautiful. You wouldn't believe it."

"Dad, it sounds perfect."

"There's one problem with the place, though, Sammy," the father whispers. "They won't let you fart."

Aunt Jean is rattling along in her car when she gets a flat tire. Being an independent woman, she jacks up the car and undoes the nuts and bolts, but as she is pulling the tire off, she loses her balance and falls backwards onto the hubcap holding the hardware. It rolls right down into a storm sewer.

This entire incident occurs outside an insane asylum and happens to

Q: Why is it hard to play cards in the jungle?

A: There are too many cheetahs!

Q: Why did the jazz musician like the wooden board?

A: Because it had a nice groove in it.

Q: What is a baby's motto?

A: If at first you don't succeed, cry, cry again!

A backward poet writes inverse.

be observed by a patient watching carefully through an open but barred window.

"Listen, lady," he calls out, "just use one bolt from each of the other three tires. They'll be plenty strong enough to get you to the gas station."

"Quick thinking," replies Aunt Jean admiringly. "Now, why on earth is a bright boy like you stuck in that place?"

"Lady, I may be crazy, but I'm not stupid."

Q: What do you get when you cross a midget with a computer?

A: A short circuit.

Q: Why do barbers make good drivers?

A: Because they know all the short cuts.

A farmer's son is returning from the market with the crate of chickens his father has entrusted to him, when all of a sudden the box falls and breaks open. Chickens scurry off in different directions, but the determined boy walks all over the neighbourhood scooping up the birds and returning them to the crate. Hoping he has found them all, the boy reluctantly returns home, anticipating the worst.

"Pa, the chickens got loose," the boy confesses sadly, "but I managed to find all 12 of them."

"Well, you did real good, son," the farmer beams. "You left with seven."

Q: What would you call the definition of surprise?

A: A fart with a lump in it.

Q: Why did the algae marry the fungus?

A: They took a lichen to each other.

## CHAPTER THIRTEEN

# Riddles, Rhymes and Brain Food

## Kid Wisdom

Never trust your dog to guard your dinner.

When your mom is mad at your dad, never let her brush your hair.

Not even your dog will eat your broccoli.

Don't sweat the petty things, and don't pet the sweaty things.

Never spit on a roller coaster.

Never dare your little brother to paint the family car.

Stay away from Brussels sprouts.

Home is where the house is.

When you want something expensive, ask your grandparents.

Wear a hat when feeding seagulls.

Sleep in your clothes so you'll be dressed in the morning.

Never try to hide a piece of broccoli in a glass of milk.

Don't flush the toilet when your dad is in the shower.

Never ask for anything that costs more than five dollars when your parents are doing taxes.

Don't pick on your sister when she's holding a baseball bat.

Listen to your brain. It has a lot of information.

When you get a bad grade in school, show it to your mom when she's on the phone.

Never try to baptize a cat.

Beware of cafeteria food when it looks like it's moving.

Never tell your little brother that you're not going to do what your mom told you to do.

## Letter from Abroad

Dear Timothy,

Hi, Hawaii! I've been Suffern from a vague Malaysia from all this Russian around. I'm weak and Congo on much longer. Otherwise, Havana good time. Alaska doctor about it when I get Nome.

Irish you were here, but Abyssinia soon!

Love, Jen

Q: How can you prove that a horse has six legs?

A: A horse has four legs (forelegs) in front and two behind.

Joe: "Did you hear the joke about the three deep holes drilled in the ground?"

Mike: "No, I didn't."

Joe: "Well...well... well."

"Do you file your nails?" Nancy asks her friend.
"No, I throw them away," replies Jenna.

"Will February March?" says the colonel.
"No, but April May," replies the private.

Q: Why do people tremble with fear when someone comes into a bank carrying a viola case?

A: They think he's carrying a viola and might be about to use it.

Mother: "Why on earth did you swallow the money I gave you?"

Little Johnny: "You said it was my lunch money."

I poured spot remover on my dog; now he's gone.

Two antennas met on a roof, fell in love and got married. The ceremony wasn't much, but the reception was excellent.

Pronounced as one letter,
And written with three,
Two letters there are,
And two only in me.
I'm double, I'm single,
I'm black, blue, and gray,
I'm read from both ends,
And the same either way.
What am I?

*An eye.*

In a marble hall white as milk
Lined with skin as soft as silk
Within a fountain crystal-clear
A golden apple doth appear.
No doors there are to this stronghold,
Yet thieves break in to steal its gold.
What is it?

*An egg.*

—*Mother Goose*

## Other Ways to Say "Stupid"

Not the sharpest knife in the drawer.

A few clowns short of a circus.

A few fries short of a Happy Meal.

Dumber than a box of hair.

A few peas short of a casserole.

Doesn't have all his Cornflakes in one box.

The wheel's spinning, but the hamster's dead.

One Fruit Loop shy of a full bowl.

One taco short of a combo plate.

The cheese slid off his cracker.

Body by Fisher, brains by Mattel.

Couldn't pour water out of a boot with instructions on the heel.

Smart as bait.

Her sewing machine's out of thread.

His belt doesn't go through all the loops.

No grain in that silo.

Skylight leaks a little.

Surfing in Nebraska.

Too much yardage between the goalposts.

# The Oxymoron List

Act naturally

Found missing

Advanced basic

Airline food

Good grief

Same difference

Almost exactly

Alone together

Living dead

Small crowd

Soft rock

Butt head

New classic

Sweet sorrow

Childproof

Taped live

Clearly misunderstood

Peace force

Extinct Life

Plastic glasses

Terribly pleased

Political science

Definite maybe

Pretty ugly

Working vacation

All about but cannot be seen,
Can be captured, cannot be held,
No throat, but can be heard.
What is it?

*The wind.*

If you break me,
I do not stop working.
If you touch me,
I may be snared.
If you lose me,
Nothing will matter.
What am I?

*My heart.*

I am the fountain from which no one can drink. For many I am considered a necessary link. Like gold to all I am sought for but my continued death brings wealth for all to want more. What am I?

*Oil.*

If you want to kiss your hunny, but her nose is kinda runny, you may think it's funny, but it's snot!

# Kid Wisdom

No one is listening until you fart.

Never try to teach a pig to sing. It wastes your time and annoys the pig.

If you live in a glass house, you should change clothes in the basement.

People will believe anything if you whisper it.

To keep milk from turning sour, keep it in the cow.

One of the main causes of dust is janitors.

There is a tremendous weight pushing down on the centre of the earth because so many people are stomping around there these days.

Water vapour gets together in a big cloud. When it gets big enough to be called a drop, it does.

Never lick a steak knife.

Don't believe in superstition; it brings bad luck.

Shin: a device for finding furniture in the dark.

If Wile E. Coyote had enough money to buy all that Acme junk, why didn't he just buy dinner?

Did you ever notice that when you blow in a dog's face, he gets mad at you, but when you take him on a car ride, he can't wait to stick his head out the window into the wind?

Who was the first person to look at a cow and say, "I think I'll squeeze these dangly things here, and drink whatever comes out?"

Q: Why don't penguins like rock music?

A: They only like sole.

## CHAPTER FOURTEEN

# Knock-Joke-a-palooza

Did you hear the riddle about the front door?

No, but I bet it's a knock-knock joke!

Knock knock!
Who's there?
Andi!
Andi who?
Andi will always love youuuuuu!

Knock knock!
Who's there?
Abbey!
Abbey who?
Abbey stung me on the nose!

Knock knock!
Who's there?
Amahl!
Amahl who?
Amahl shook up!

Knock knock!
Who's there?
Dishes!
Dishes who?
Dishes a very bad joke!

Knock knock!
Who's there?
Abba!
Abba who?
Abba banana!

Knock knock!
Who's there?
Interrupting cow!
Interrupt...
MOOOOOOOO!

Knock knock!
Who's there?
U-8!
U-8 who?
U-8 my lunch!

Knock knock!
Who's there?
Canoe!
Canoe who?
Canoe help me with my homework,
I'm stuck!

Knock knock!
Who's there?
Tank!
Tank who?
My pleasure!

Knock knock!
Who's there?
Radio!
Radio who?
Radio not, here I come!

Knock knock!
Who's there?
Reed!
Reed who?
Reed between the lines!

Knock knock!
Who's there?
Kanga!
Kanga who?
No, kangaroo!

Knock knock!
Who's there?
Kyoto!
Kyoto who?
Kyoto jail: do not pass go; do not collect $200!

Knock knock!
Who's there!
Dynamite!
Dynamite who?
Dynamite if you ask her nicely!

Knock knock!
Who's there?
Ya!
Ya who?
I didn't know you were a cowboy!

Knock knock!
Who's there?
Disease!
Disease who?
Disease clothes fit you?

Knock knock!
Who's there?
Yukon!
Yukon who?
Yukon leave and come back at a reasonable time!

Knock knock!
Who's there?
Yuri!
Yuri who?
Yuri great friend!

Knock knock!
Who's there?
Dan!
Dan who?
Dan Druff!

Knock knock!
Who's there?
Denial!
Denial who?
Denial's in Egypt, but I'm here!

Knock knock!
Who's there?
Seoul!
Seoul who?
Seoul food!

Knock knock!
Who's there?
Paine!
Paine who?
Paine in the neck!

Knock knock!
Who's there?
Parton!
Parton who?
Parton my French!

Knock knock!
Who's there?
Pen!
Pen who?
Pen-t up emotions!

Knock knock!
Who's there?
Taipei!
Taipei who?
Taipei 60 words a minute is fast!

Knock knock!
Who's there?
Saturn!
Saturn who?
Saturnday Night Fever!

Knock knock!
Who's there?
Tibet!
Tibet who?
Early Tibet and early to rise!

Knock knock!
Who's there?
Sal!
Sal who?
Sa-long way to India!

Knock knock!
Who's there?
Senta!
Senta who?
Senta letter by Express Mail!

Knock knock!
Who's there?
Willa!
Willa who?
Willa you marry me!

Knock knock!
Who's there?
Wilma!
Wilma who?
Wilma dreams come true?

Knock knock!
Who's there?
Utah!
Utah who?
Utah told me to knock!

Knock knock!
Who's there?
I-8!
I-8 who?
I-8 lunch already. Is dinner ready?

Knock knock!
Who's there?
Ivy!
Ivy who?
Ivy got you under my skin!

Knock knock!
Who's there?
Galway!
Galway who?
Galway, you're annoying me!

Knock knock!
Who's there?
Gopher!
Gopher who?
Gopher broke!

Knock knock!
Who's there?
Gwenna!
Gwenna who?
Gwenna phone rings, answer it!

Knock knock!
Who's there?
Xavier!
Xavier who?
Xavier money for a rainy day!

Knock knock!
Who's there?
Amana!
Amana who?
Amana bad mood!

Knock knock!
Who's there?
Heaven!
Heaven who?
Heaven seen you in ages!

Knock knock!
Who's there?
Toucan!
Toucan who?
Toucan play at this game!

Knock knock!
Who's there?
Hollis!
Hollis who?
Hollis forgiven, come back home!

Knock knock!
Who's there?
Idaho!
Idaho who?
Idaho'd the whole garden, but I was
tired!

Knock knock!
Who's there?
Tunis!
Tunis who?
Tunis company, three's a crowd!

Knock knock!
Who's there?
Jaguar!
Jaguar who?
Jaguar nimble, Jaguar quick!

Knock knock!
Who's there?
Jamaica!
Jamaica who?
Jamaica mistake?

Knock knock!
Who's there?
Kay!
Kay who?
Kay sera sera!

Knock knock!
Who's there?
Wade!
Wade who?
Wade till next time!

Knock knock!
Who's there?
Handel!
Handel who?
Handel with care!

Knock knock!
Who's there?
Uruguay!
Uruguay who?
You go Uruguay and I'll go mine!

Knock knock!
Who's there?
Tyson!
Tyson who?
Tyson of this on for size!

Knock knock!
Who's there?
Value!
Value who?
Value be my Valentine?

Knock knock!
Who's there?
Hank!
Hank who?
Hank you!

Knock knock!
Who's there?
Handsome!
Handsome who?
Handsome of the money to me!

Knock knock!
Who's there?
Hans!
Hans who?
Hans off the table!

Knock knock!
Who's there?
Hyman!
Hyman who?
Hyman in the mood for dancin'!

Knock knock!
Who's there?
Hutch!
Hutch who?
Bless you, and I'm out of tissues!

Knock knock!
Who's there?
Iguana!
Iguana who?
Iguana hold your hand!

Knock knock!
Who's there?
Iris!
Iris who?
Iris you were here!

Knock knock!
Who's there?
Kipper!
Kipper who?
Kipper hands to yourself!

Knock knock!
Who's there?
Koch!
Koch who?
Koch you in the act!

Knock knock!
Who's there?
Laos!
Laos who?
Laos and found!

Knock knock!
Who's there?
Leaf!
Leaf who?
Leaf me alone!

Knock knock!
Who's there?
Beets!
Beets who?
Beets me!

Knock knock!
Who's there?
Bette-lou!
Bette-lou who?
Bette-lou a few pounds!

Knock knock!
Who's there?
May!
May who?
Maybe it's a friend at the door!

Knock knock!
Who's there?
Max!
Max who?
Max no difference. Open the door!

Knock knock!
Who's there?
Meg!
Meg who?
Meg up your mind!

Knock knock!
Who's there?
Isaac!
Isaac who?
Isaac coming out?

Knock knock!
Who's there?
Isabella!
Isabella who?
Isabella out of order?

Knock knock!
Who's there?
Isabelle!
Isabelle who?
Isabelle necessary on a bicycle?

Knock knock!
Who's there?
Isadore!
Isadore who?
Isadore locked? I can't get in!

Knock knock!
Who's there?
Alpaca!
Alpaca who?
Alpaca the food, and you bring the water!

## CHAPTER FIFTEEN

# Mix Up

Two elderly couples are enjoying friendly conversation when one of the men asks the other, "Fred, how was the memory clinic you went to last month?"

"Outstanding," Fred replies. "They taught us all the latest psychological techniques—visualization, association—it has made a big difference for me."

"That's great! What was the name of that clinic?"

Fred's mind goes blank. He thinks and thinks but can't remember. Then he smiles and says, "What do you call that flower with the long stem and thorns?"

"You mean a rose?"

"Yes, that's it!" He turns to his wife and says, "Rose, what was the name of that clinic?"

An efficiency expert is concluding his lecture with a note of caution: "You don't want to try these techniques at home."

"Why not?" asks somebody in the audience.

"I watched my wife's routine at breakfast for years," the expert explains. "She made a lot of trips between the refrigerator, stove, table and cabinets, often carrying a single item at a time. One day, I said to her, 'Hon, why don't you try carrying several things at once?'"

"Did it save time?" the audience member asks.

> Q  What do you call a man with no arms and no legs who is in the pool?
>
> A:  Bob.

"Actually, yes," replies the expert. "It used to take her 20 minutes to make breakfast. Now I do it in seven."

Bob: "Hey, Bill, did you hear about the artists who held a competition?"

Bill: "No. How did it turn out?"

Bob: "It was a draw."

An American man, a Russian man and an African man are in a hot-air balloon together. After a few minutes, the Russian man puts his hand down through the clouds. "Aaah!" he says, "we're right over my homeland."

"How can you tell?" asks the American.

"I can feel the cold air," he replies.

A few hours later, the African man puts his hand through the clouds. "Aaah, we're right over my homeland," he says.

"How do you know that?" asks the Russian.

"I can feel the heat of the desert."

Several hours later, the American puts his hand through the clouds. "Aaah, we're right over New York."

The Russian and the African are amazed. "How do you know that?" they exclaim.

The American pulls his hand up and says "My watch is missing."

Jack and Dave have been best friends for a very long time, and when they are in their 90s, Jack suddenly falls deathly ill. Dave goes to visit Jack on his deathbed, and while they reminisce about their long friendship, Dave says, "Listen, when you die, Jack, do me one favour. I want to know if there's baseball in heaven."

Jack says, "We've been friends for years. This I'll do for you." And then Jack dies.

A couple of days later, Dave is sleeping when he hears Jack's voice. The voice says, "I've got some good news and some bad news. The good news is that there's baseball in heaven."

"What's the bad news?" asks Dave.

"You're pitching on Wednesday."

Q:  Have you heard the joke about the bed?

A:  It hasn't been made up yet.

Two guys are walking through the jungle. All of a sudden, a tiger appears from a distance, running toward them. One of the guys takes out a pair of Nikes from his bag and starts to put them on.

The other guy, with a surprised look on his face, exclaims, "Do you think you will run faster than the tiger with those?"

Q: How many musicians does it take to change a light bulb?

A: One, and 10 on the guest list.

His friend replies, "I don't have to outrun the tiger. I just have to run faster than you."

Alfie has been listening to his sister practicing her singing.

"Sis," he says, "I wish you'd sing Christmas carols."

"That's nice of you, Alfie," she replies. "Why?"

"Then I'd only have to hear you once a year!"

A priest is walking down the street one day when he notices a small boy trying to press a doorbell on a house across the street. However, the boy is very small, and the doorbell is too high for him to reach.

After watching the boy's efforts for some time, the priest moves closer to the boy's position.

He steps across the street, walks up behind the little fellow and, placing his hand kindly on the child's shoulder, leans over and gives the doorbell a solid ring.

Crouching down to the child's level, the priest smiles and asks, "And now what, my little man?"

To which the boy replies, "Now, we run!"

Teacher: "What is an island?"

Student: "A piece of land surrounded by water, except on one side."

Teacher: "On one side?"

Student: "Yes, on top!"

One morning, a mother and her three children are out working in the field. One of her young daughters goes up to her and says, "Mama, why is my name Daisy?"

Her mother says, "Well, sweetie, when you were born, a daisy fell on your head."

Her daughter trots off, satisfied.

The next day, they are all out in the field again. The second daughter goes up to her mother and says, "Mama, why is my name Rose?"

"Well, honey, when you were born, a rose fell on your head."

Her daughter is happy with that answer and continues working.

The next day, they all go out into the field again to work. The son goes up to his mother and says, "GLUPHABABABLUGHARDTHYPOGHHH!"

And the mother says, "Good morning, Brick!"

A man named José goes to America to watch the Yankees play the Red Socks. When he gets the ticket, it says "Nosebleed Section." He doesn't care what section he is in. At the beginning of the game, everyone stands for the national anthem.

When José gets home, he says, "Mama, they made a song in America just for me."

"How does it go?" ask his mother.

"It goes 'José can you see!'"

Q: What do you call a boomerang that doesn't work?

A: A stick.

## True Story

A woman comes home to find her husband in the kitchen shaking frantically, almost in a frenzy. She sees he has some kind of wire running from his waist towards the electric kettle. Intending to jolt him away from the deadly current, she whacks him with a handy plank of wood, breaking his arm in two places. Up to that moment, he had been happily listening to his iPod.

## The Top Rejected Titles for Children's Books

1. *The Magical World Inside the Abandoned Refrigerator*

2. *Where to Find the Toys in the Oven*

3. *101 Games to Play in the Road*

4. *Homemade Fireworks Using a Bathtub, a Blowdryer and a Fork*

5. *Your Nightmares Are Real*

6. *Monsters Killed Grandpa*

7. *All Guns Squirt Water*

8. *How Fun It Is to Tie a Squirrel to a Kite*

9. *If It's Storming Out, the Best Place to Find Shelter Is Under a Tree*

## Grandma and Grandpa

An elderly couple is sitting on a park bench in front of a large pond. On the other side of the pond are vendors selling all types of snacks. The wife turns to her hubby and says, "I could really go for an ice cream cone."

Hubby replies, "Well, I'll go get you one."

Wife says, "But you'll forget. You'd better write it down."

Hubby replies, "No, I won't. What do you want?"

Wife says, "Get me a strawberry cone with chocolate sprinkles."

Hubby replies, "Okay, strawberry cone with chocolate sprinkles. See, I'll remember."

Several hours pass and, finally, the man returns.

The wife asks him, "What took you so long, did you get lost?"

The hubby replies, "No, and I got what you wanted."

The wife opens the bag to discover a cheeseburger and fries.

Wife says, "I knew you should have written it down."

Hubby says, "What do you mean? Isn't everything in there?"

Q: What happens when you play country music backwards?

A: Your dog comes back, you get your truck back, your momma gets out of jail...

The wife replies, "No, it's not! Look, you forgot the pickles!"

Two elderly women are enjoying the sunshine on a park bench in Victoria. They have been meeting in the park every sunny day for over 12 years, chatting and enjoying each other's company.

One day, the younger of the two women turns to the other and says, "Please don't be angry with me, dear, but I'm embarrassed. After all these years, what is your name? I'm trying to remember, but I just can't."

The older friend stares at her, looking very distressed, and says nothing for two minutes. Then, finally, with tearful eyes, she says, "How soon do you have to know?"

A little boy goes up to his father and asks, "Daddy, is God a man or a woman?"

"Both, son. God is both."

After a while, the kid asks, "Daddy, is God black or white?"

"Both, son, both."

The child thinks for a few minutes and then says, "Daddy, is Michael Jackson God?"

A man from Alberta leaves the snowy streets of Edmonton for a vacation in Florida. His wife is on a business trip and plans to meet him there the next day. When he reaches his hotel, the man decides to send his wife a quick e-mail. Unable to find the scrap of paper on which he had written her e-mail address, he types it in as best he can from memory. Unfortunately, he misses one letter, and his note is

> Q:  How do crazy people go through the forest?
> A:  They take the psycho path.

directed instead to an elderly preacher's wife whose husband had passed away only the day before. When the grieving widow checks her e-mail, she takes one look at the monitor, lets out a piercing scream and falls to the floor, dead.

At the sound, her family rushes into the room and sees this note on the screen:

*Dearest Wife,*

*Just got checked in. Everything prepared for your arrival tomorrow.*

*Your Loving Husband.*

*PS. Sure is hot down here.*

In a small neighbourhood, there are two brothers, 8 and 10 years old, who are very mischievous. Whatever goes wrong in the neighbourhood, it nearly always turns out that they had a hand in it. The boys' parents do not know how to control them, but after hearing about a priest who works with troubled boys, the mother suggests to her husband that they ask the priest to talk to the two.

Q: Why are movie stars so cool?

A: Because they have many fans!

The mother goes to see the priest and makes her request. The priest agrees but says he wants to see the younger boy first. So, the mother sends him to the priest.

The priest sits the boy down across from himself at a huge, impressive desk. For about five minutes, they just sit and stare at each other. Finally, the priest points his forefinger at the boy and asks, "Where is God?"

The boy looks under the desk, in the corners of the room, all around, but says nothing.

Again, louder, the priest points at the boy and asks, "Where is God?"

Again, the boy looks all around the room but says nothing.

A third time, in a louder, firmer voice, the priest leans far across the desk and puts his forefinger almost to the boy's nose, and asks, "Where is God?"

The boy panics and runs all the way home. Finding his brother, he drags him upstairs to their room and into the closet, where they usually plot their mischief, and says, "We are in big trouble!"

The older boy asks, "What do you mean, big trouble?"

His brother replies, "God is missing, and they think we did it!"

Farmer Joe is returning from town with his cow, Bessy, and his dog, Rusty, in the back of his truck. On a really slick section of hillside with a steep drop of 50 metres, he loses control of his truck and falls off the hillside. As the truck rolls over several times, the dog and cow are thrown down the slope.

All survive the tumble, but the farmer, unfortunately, is underneath the truck and in severe pain with a broken leg, several cracked ribs and a broken wrist and arm.

It so happens that a police officer comes along. Treading his way carefully down the slope, he comes upon the cow first. She has suffered a broken leg. Knowing how much pain she is in, the officer takes out his gun and puts Bessy out of her misery. He proceeds down the slope and comes across Rusty, crawling along, dragging two broken legs. He has been hit pretty hard. Again, the officer unholsters his gun and does the kindest thing.

> Q: Why is it so cold at Christmas?
>
> A: Because it's in Decembrrrrr.

He then continues on to Farmer Joe. The officer stares down at him and says, "Are you in much pain?"

Farmer Joe, eyeing the gun on the officer's hip, quickly replies, "Never felt better!"

In the days when tall wooden ships sailed the seas, there's one ship sailing during a war.

One morning, the lookout shouts, "Enemy ship on the horizon!"

The captain says to his junior officer, "Get me my red shirt."

The junior officer does as his captain orders.

Though the battle is long, the captain and his crew manage to defeat the enemy.

Later that day, the lookout shouts, "Two enemy ships on the horizon!"

As before, the captain says to his junior officer, "Get me my red shirt." And, as before, the junior officer does as his captain asks.

The battle takes the rest of the day to fight, and again they manage to defeat the enemy ships.

The evening comes, and the junior officer asks his captain, "Sir, why, before every battle, do you ask for your red shirt?"

The captain replies, "Well, if I am wounded in battle, the blood will not show, and the crew will continue to fight."

The crew is listening, and they are impressed. They have a brave captain.

The next morning, the lookout shouts, "Ten enemy ships on the horizon!"

The junior officer looks at his captain, waiting for the usual orders. The captain says to his junior officer, "Officer, get me my brown pants!"

A motorist, driving by an Alberta ranch, hits and kills a calf that is crossing the road. The driver goes to the owner of the calf and explains what has happened. He then asks what the animal was worth.

"Oh, about $200 today," says the rancher. "But in six years, it would have been worth $900. So $900 is what I'm out."

The motorist sits down and writes out a cheque and hands it to the farmer.

"Here is a cheque for $900," he says. "It's post-dated six years from now."

## Inspiring Music at Church

A minister is preoccupied with thoughts of how he is going to ask the congregation to come up with more money for repairs to the church building.

Therefore, he is annoyed to find that the regular organist is sick and a substitute had been brought in at the last minute. The substitute wants to know what to play.

"Here's a copy of the service," the minister says impatiently. "But you'll have to think of something to play after I make the announcement about the finances."

In a democracy, it's your vote that counts. In feudalism, it's your count that votes.

During the service, the minister pauses and says, "Brothers and sisters, we are in great difficulty. The roof repairs cost twice as much as we expected, and we need $4000 more. Any of you who can pledge $100 or more, please stand up."

At that moment, the substitute organist plays the national anthem.

Joe: "My big brother who joined the army is in the hospital."

Bill: "What happened to him?"

Joe: "He's a karate expert. The first time he saluted, he knocked himself out."

A woman walks into a high-end dress store and says to the owner, "I'm the greatest salesperson ever. And I want a job."

"That's quite a claim," the owner responds, "but unfortunately, I don't have any openings."

Undaunted, the woman says, "How many dresses does your best employee sell in a day?"

"Five or six," the owner replies.

Without thinking, the woman says, "I'll sell 12 without pay or commission, just to show how good I am."

The soldier who survived mustard gas and pepper spray is now a seasoned veteran.

The owner, knowing she can't lose, agrees. And, indeed, just an hour before closing, the new salesperson has sold 18 dresses.

"Do I get the job now?" she asks.

"I've got one more test for you," the owner says. She goes back into the storeroom and returns with the most hideous dress imaginable. "Sell this dress by the time the store closes tonight, and you've got a job."

Forty-five minutes later, the woman goes into the owner's office and throws down the sales receipt.

> Q: Did you hear about the rock 'n' roll singer who wore a hearing aid for four years?
>
> A: He found out he only needed a haircut.

"I'm impressed," the owner admits in amazement. "You've got the job. But how on earth did you convince somebody to buy that dress?"

"Getting the woman to buy it wasn't the problem. The hard part was fooling her seeing-eye dog."

The top salesman at a toothbrush company is asked by his boss how he manages to sell so many toothbrushes.

The salesman replies, "It's easy," and he pulls out his card table, setting his display of toothbrushes on top. He says to his boss, "I lay the brushes out like this, and then I put out some potato chips and dip to draw in the customers." He then lays out the chips and dip.

His boss says, "That's a very innovative approach," as he takes one of the chips, dips it and puts it in his mouth. "Yuck, this tastes terrible!" he yells.

The salesman replies, "It does? Want to buy a toothbrush?"

# Letters to God

Dear God: Thank you for the baby brother, but what I prayed for was a puppy.

Dear God: My brother is a rat. You should give him a tail. Ha ha.

Dear God: Of all the people who work for you, I like Noah and David the best.

Dear God: My brother told me about being born, but it doesn't sound right. They're just kidding, aren't they?

Dear God: I would like to live 900 years like the guy in the Bible.

Dear God: I didn't think orange went with purple until I saw the sunset you made on Tuesday. That was cool!

Dear God: In school they told us what you do. Who does it when you are on vacation?

Dear God: Who draws the lines around the countries?

Dear God: What does it mean you are "a Jealous God"? I thought you had everything.

Dear God: It rained for our whole vacation and is my father ever mad! He said some things about you that people are not supposed to say, but I hope you will not hurt him anyway. Your friend (but I am not going to tell you who I am).

Dear God: Instead of letting people die and having to make new ones, why don't you just keep the ones you have?

Dear God: If you watch me in church on Sunday, I'll show you my new shoes.

Dear God: Maybe Cain and Abel would not have killed each other so much if they'd had their own rooms. That's what my mom did for my brother and me.

Dear God: I bet it is very hard for you to love all of everybody in the whole world. There are only four people in our family, and I'm having a hard time loving all of them.

Dear God: Are you really invisible or is it just a trick?

Dear God: Is it true my father won't get into heaven if he uses his bowling words in the house?

Dear God: Did you mean for the giraffe to look like that, or was it an accident?

Dear God: I went to this wedding, and they kissed right in the church. Is that okay?

## Also from
## FOLKLORE PUBLISHING...

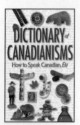

### DICTIONARY OF CANADIANISMS
How to Speak Canadian, Eh!
by Geordie Telfer
We have a vocabulary—and a number of dialects—all our own. So, sit on the chesterfield with a plate of poutine and a glass of screech and read this tongue-in-cheek take on Canada's unofficial language.

$18.95 • ISBN: 978-1-894864-85-5 • 5.25" x 8.25" • 352 pages

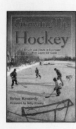

### GROWING UP HOCKEY
The Life and Times of Everyone Who Ever Loved the Game
by Brian Kennedy
foreword by Kelly Hrudey
This memoir is about the timeless magic of growing up playing hockey on the frozen lakes, rivers and ponds of northern Canada and the United States. An autobiography of anyone who ever loved the game.

$19.95 • ISBN: 978-1-894864-65-7 • 5.5" x 8.5" • 384 pages

### AMAZING ANIMALS
Inspiring Stories About the Bond Between Humans and Animals
by Janice Ryan
From squirrels that take up the house with a litter of puppies to horses that think they're human, this book is a collection of fascinating, heartwarming and humorous tales about some of the animal kingdom's amazing inhabitants.

$14.95 • ISBN: 978-1-894864-77-0 • 5.25" x 8.25" • 256 pages

Available from your local bookseller or by contacting the distributor,
Lone Pine Publishing • 1-800-661-9017
www.lonepinepublishing.com